Experiencing
Choral Music

TREBLE

Developed by

HAL•LEONARD®
CORPORATION

Mc Graw Hill Glencoe

New York, New York   Columbus, Ohio   Chicago, Illinois   Peoria, Illinois   Woodland Hills, California

 **Glencoe**

The *McGraw·Hill* Companies

Printed in the United States of America.

Send all inquiries to:
Glencoe/McGraw-Hill
21600 Oxnard Street, Suite 500
Woodland Hills, CA 91367

ISBN 0-07-861111-3 (Student Edition)
ISBN 0-07-861112-1 (Teacher Wraparound Edition)

5 6 7 8 9   045   09 08 07 06

Credits

LEAD AUTHORS

Emily Crocker
Vice President of Choral Publications
Hal Leonard Corporation, Milwaukee, Wisconsin
Founder and Artistic Director, Milwaukee Children's Choir

Michael Jothen
Professor of Music, Program Director of Graduate Music Education
Chairperson of Music Education
Towson University, Towson, Maryland

Jan Juneau
Choral Director
Klein Collins High School
Spring, Texas

Henry H. Leck
Associate Professor and Director of Choral Activities
Butler University, Indianapolis, Indiana
Founder and Artistic Director, Indianapolis Children's Choir

Michael O'Hern
Choral Director
Lake Highlands High School
Richardson, Texas

Audrey Snyder
Composer
Eugene, Oregon

Mollie Tower
Coordinator of Choral and General Music, K-12, Retired
Austin, Texas

AUTHORS

Anne Denbow
Voice Instructor, Professional Singer/Actress
Director of Music, Holy Cross Episcopal Church
Simpsonville, South Carolina

Rollo A. Dilworth
Director of Choral Activities and Music
 Education
North Park University, Chicago, Illinois

Deidre Douglas
Choral Director
Aragon Middle School, Houston, Texas

Ruth E. Dwyer
Associate Director and Director of Education
Indianapolis Children's Choir
Indianapolis, Indiana

Norma Freeman
Choral Director
Saline High School, Saline, Michigan

Cynthia I. Gonzales
Music Theorist
Greenville, South Carolina

Michael Mendoza
Professor of Choral Activities
New Jersey State University
Trenton, New Jersey

Thomas Parente
Associate Professor
Westminster Choir College of Rider University
Princeton, New Jersey

Barry Talley
Director of Fine Arts and Choral Director
Deer Park ISD, Deer Park, Texas

CONTRIBUTING AUTHORS

Debbie Daniel
Choral Director, Webb Middle School
Garland, Texas

Roger Emerson
Composer/Arranger
Mount Shasta, California

Kari Gilbertson
Choral Director, Forest Meadow Junior High
Richardson, Texas

Tim McDonald
Creative Director, Music Theatre International
New York, New York

Christopher W. Peterson
Assistant Professor of Music Education (Choral)
University of Wisconsin-Milwaukee
Milwaukee, Wisconsin

Kirby Shaw
Composer/Arranger
Ashland, Oregon

Stephen Zegree
Professor of Music
Western Michigan State University
Kalamazoo, Michigan

EDITORIAL

Linda Rann
Senior Editor
Hal Leonard Corporation
Milwaukee, Wisconsin

Stacey Nordmeyer
Choral Editor
Hal Leonard Corporation
Milwaukee, Wisconsin

Table of Contents

Lessons

Music & History

Choral Library

TO THE STUDENT

Welcome to choir!

By singing in the choir, you have chosen to be a part of an exciting and rewarding adventure. The benefits of being in choir are many. Basically, singing is fun. It provides an expressive way of sharing your feelings and emotions. Through choir, you will have friends that share a common interest with you. You will experience the joy of making beautiful music together. Choir provides the opportunity to develop your interpersonal skills. It takes teamwork and cooperation to sing together, and you must learn how to work with others. As you critique your individual and group performances, you can improve your ability to analyze and communicate your thoughts clearly.

Even if your do not pursue a music career, music can be an important part of your life. There are many avocational opportunities in music. **Avocational** means *not related to a job or career*. Singing as a hobby can provide you with personal enjoyment, enrich your life, and teach you life skills. Singing is something you can do for the rest of your life.

In this course, you will be presented with the basic skills of vocal production and music literacy. You will be exposed to songs from different cultures, songs in many different styles and languages, and songs from various historical periods. You will discover connections between music and the other arts. Guidelines for becoming a better singer and choir member include:

- Come to class prepared to learn.

- Respect the efforts of others.

- Work daily to improve your sight-singing skills.

- Sing expressively at all times.

- Have fun singing.

This book was written to provide you with a meaningful choral experience. Take advantage of the knowledge and opportunities offered here. Your exciting adventure of experiencing choral music is about to begin!

Lessons

Lessons for the Beginning of the Year

Lessons for Mid-Winter

Lessons for Concert/Festival

Red River Dances

Composer: American Folk Songs, arranged by Cristi Cary Miller
Text: Traditional
Voicing: 2-Part

VOCABULARY

legato

diction

folk song

interval

parallel thirds

 **SPOTLIGHT**

To learn more about diction, see page 13.

Focus

- Sing music in contrasting styles.
- Read and perform music with parallel thirds.
- Perform American folk music.

Getting Started

"Red River Dances" is a medley of American folk songs, including "The Red River Valley," "Chicken On The Fence Post," and "Old Joe Clark." "Red River Valley" is lyrical, and you will need a steady flow of breath to help create a **legato**, or *a connected and sustained,* vocal line. In contrast, "Chicken On The Fence Post" and "Old Joe Clark" are rhythmically energetic and will require special attention to **diction**, or *the pronunciation of words while singing.* As you learn "Red River Dances," think of ways you can perform these pieces to show this contrast.

◆ History and Culture

Folk songs are *songs that were originally passed down from generation to generation through oral tradition and often describe a certain place or event.* The melody to "The Red River Valley," though popular with the American cowboy, originated in New York State. Across the country, this song refers to different places. In the South, it speaks of the river that borders Oklahoma and Texas. However, in the North, this song can refer to the river that flows from North Dakota into Canada. "Old Joe Clark" tells exaggerated tales from the life of Joseph Clark, a Kentucky mountain man and Civil War veteran. "Chicken On The Fence Post" is an example of a Southwestern play-party song, and it was a favorite among young people. As the name implies, a play-party song is one in which people sing as they play a game.

Links to Learning

◆ Vocal

Read and perform the following example to establish the key of F major and to prepare you to sing the opening section of "Red River Dances."

sol do mi   do mi sol   mi sol mi   sol mi do   mi do sol   do

◆ Theory

An **interval** is *the distance between two different notes or pitches*. When two pitches are three notes apart on the staff, the interval is called a third. **Parallel thirds** refer to *the parallel motion of a group of notes that are the interval of a third part*. Sing the following example to develop the ability to sing in parallel thirds.

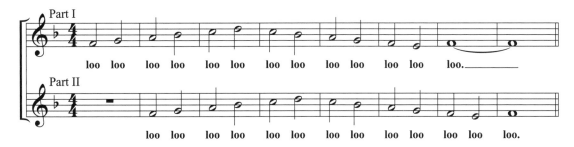

Evaluation

Demonstrate how well you have learned the skills and concepts featured in the lesson "Red River Dances" by completing the following:

• Record or videotape your choir singing "Red River Dances." As a choir, review the recording. How smooth are the legato portions of the piece? How clear is your choir's diction?

• As a duet with one person on a part, sing measures 21–37 to show that you can sing in parallel thirds. How well were you able to sing in tune?

Red River Dances

The Red River Valley • Chicken On The Fence Post • Old Joe Clark

For 2-Part and Piano

Arranged by
CRISTI CARY MILLER

American Folk Songs

6 THE RED RIVER VALLEY
Traditional American Cowboy Song

From this val - ley they say you are go - ing.

From this val - ley they say you are go - ing.

I shall miss your bright eyes and sweet smile. ____

I shall miss your bright eyes and sweet smile. ____

American Folk Song

OLD JOE CLARK
Tennessee Folk Song

Round and a-round, I say. He'd fol-low me ten

Chick-en on the fence post; can't dance, Jo-sie. Chick-en on the fence post;

94

thou-sand miles to hear my fid-dle play.

can't dance, Jo-sie. Hel-lo Su-san,

97

Old Joe Clark! Hear my fid-dle play! Yeow!

Old Joe Clark!_____ Hear my fid-dle play! Yeow!

100

SPOTLIGHT

Diction

Singing is a form of communication. To communicate well while singing, you must not only form your vowels correctly, but also say your consonants as clearly and cleanly as possible.

There are two kinds of consonants: voiced and unvoiced. Consonants that require the use of the voice along with the **articulators** *(lips, teeth, tongue, and other parts of the mouth and throat)* are called voiced consonants. If you place your hand on your throat, you can actually feel your voice box vibrate while producing them. Unvoiced consonant sounds are made with the articulators only.

In each pair below, the first word contains a voiced consonant while the second word contains an unvoiced consonant. Speak the following word pairs, then sing them on any pitch. When singing, make sure the voiced consonant is on the same pitch as the vowel.

Voiced:	Unvoiced Consonants:	More Voiced Consonants:
[b] bay	[p] pay	[l] lip
[d] den	[t] ten	[m] mice
[g] goat	[k] coat	[n] nice
[dʒ] jeer	[ʧ] cheer	[j] yell
[z] zero	[s] scenic	[r] red
[ʒ] fusion	[ʃ] shun	
[ð] there	[θ] therapy	More Unvoiced Consonants:
[v] vine	[f] fine	[h] have
[w] wince	[hw] whim	

The American "r" requires special treatment in classical choral singing. To sing an American "r" at the end of a syllable following a vowel, sing the vowel with your teeth apart and jaw open. In some formal sacred music and English texts, you may need to flip or roll the "r." For most other instances, sing the "r" on pitch, then open to the following vowel quickly.

Dona Nobis Pacem

Composer: Mary Lynn Lightfoot
Text: Traditional Latin
Voicing: 2-Part

VOCABULARY

countermelody

mass

syllabic stress

crescendo

decrescendo

 SPOTLIGHT

To learn more about vowels, see page 21.

Focus

- Perform music with correct syllabic stress.
- Read, write and perform rhythmic patterns accurately.

Getting Started

Peppermint, spearmint and wintergreen are great flavors for chewing gum. But if you put two mint flavors together, the taste will be even stronger. The Wrigley Company of Chicago, Illinois, figured this out in 1914 and created Doublemint® gum. For years, composers have known that combining two melodies into one song can create a stronger effect. And don't forget, gum and chorus singers should never mix.

◆ History and Culture

This setting of "Dona Nobis Pacem" is a contemporary example of two musical ideas, the melody and a countermelody, combined together. A **countermelody** is *a separate vocal line that supports and contrasts the primary melody.*

The Latin words *dona nobis pacem* can be translated as "give us peace." These words have been set to music for many centuries and come from one section of the mass. A **mass** is *a religious service of prayers and ceremonies.* Though not a modern spoken language, Latin, with its pure vowels, is a favorite of singers.

Singing in Latin will give you the opportunity to learn **syllabic stress,** or *the stressing of one syllable over another.* For example, with the word "music," you would sing "MU-sic," rather than "mu-SIC." Discuss where you would place the syllabic stress on the words "soprano," "alto," and "September."

Links to Learning

◆ Vocal

Perform the following example to practice singing with syllabic stress. In each phrase, place a slight stress on the first syllable of "nobis." Observe each **crescendo** or ⎯◁ *(a dynamic marking that indicates to gradually sing louder)* and **decrescendo** or ▷⎯ *(a dynamic marking that indicates to gradually sing softer)* to indicate syllabic stress.

Do-na NO-bis,　do-na NO-bis,　do-na NO-bis PA - cem.　Do-na

NO - bis,　do - na NO - bis　do-na NO - bis PA - cem.

◆ Theory

Read and pat in the palm of your hand the following rhythmic patterns. For the rests, silently mouth the word "beat" and mime its clap. For the half notes, slide the pat over two beats. With a classmate, perform two different patterns at the same time.

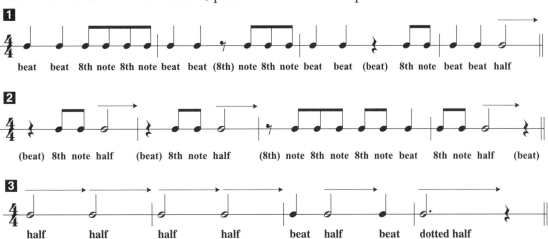

1 beat beat 8th note 8th note beat beat (8th) note 8th note beat beat (beat) 8th note beat beat half

2 (beat) 8th note half (beat) 8th note half (8th) note 8th note 8th note beat 8th note half (beat)

3 half half half half beat half beat dotted half

Evaluation

Demonstrate how well you have learned the skills and concepts featured in the lesson "Dona Nobis Pacem" by completing the following.

- Sing measures 13–21 of "Dona Nobis Pacem" using correct syllabic stress. Evaluate how well you were able to apply this skill.

- Compose your own four-measure rhythmic pattern using half notes, quarter notes, eighth notes, and their corresponding rests. Share with a classmate and check each other's work.

For my cousin, Dr. Sara Crump

Dona Nobis Pacem

For 2-Part and Piano

Traditional Latin

Music by
MARY LYNN LIGHTFOOT

SPOTLIGHT

Vowels

The style of a given piece of music dictates how we should pronounce the words. If we are singing a more formal, classical piece, then we need to form taller vowels as in very proper English. If we are singing in a jazz or pop style, then we should pronounce the words in a more relaxed, conversational way. To get the feeling of taller vowels for classical singing, do the following:

- Let your jaw gently drop down and back as if it were on a hinge.
- Place your hands on your cheeks beside the corners of your mouth.
- Sigh on an *ah* [ɑ] vowel sound, but do not spread the corners of your mouth.
- Now sigh on other vowel sounds—*eh* [ɛ], *ee* [i], *oh* [o] and *oo* [u]—keeping the back of the tongue relaxed.
- As your voice goes from higher notes to lower notes, think of gently opening a tiny umbrella inside your mouth.

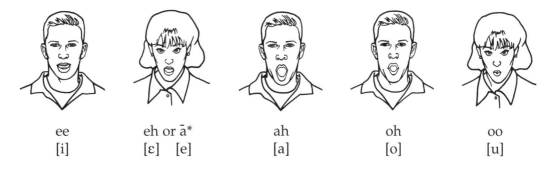

ee	eh or ā*	ah	oh	oo
[i]	[ɛ] [e]	[a]	[o]	[u]

Other vowel sounds used in singing are diphthongs. A **diphthong** is *a combination of two vowel sounds.* For example, the vowel *ay* consists of two sounds: *eh* [E] and *ee* [i]. To sing a diphthong correctly, stay on the first vowel sound for the entire length of the note, only lightly adding the second vowel sound as you move to another note or lift off the note.

I = *ah*_____(ee) [ɑi]

boy = *oh*_____(ee) [oi]

down = *ah*_____(oo) [ɑu]

*Note: This is an Italian "ā," which is one sound, and not an American "ā," which is a diphthong, or two sounds.

En Roulant Ma Boule

Composer: French-Canadian Game Song, arranged by Cristi Cary Miller
Text: Traditional
Voicing: 2-Part

VOCABULARY

jongleur

refrain

stanza

$\frac{6}{8}$ meter

 **SKILL BUILDERS**

To learn more about $\frac{6}{8}$ meter, see Intermediate Sight-Singing, *pages 114–116.*

Focus

- Relate storytelling to music.
- Read rhythmic notation in $\frac{6}{8}$ meter.
- Perform music that represents the French-Canadian culture.

Getting Started

When you hear the words "Once upon a time," you know a story is about to be told. In order for it to be interesting, the storyteller must spend time becoming familiar with the story and its characters. By adding vocal inflection, facial expression, and an occasional hand gesture, the storyteller makes the story appealing to the listener. When singing, you can add these elements to your performance to make the story you are telling come alive to your audience.

◆ History and Culture

Thought to have originated in France during the fifteenth century, "En Roulant Ma Boule" was a common jongleur song. **Jongleurs** were *entertainers who traveled from town to town during medieval times.* Often they told stories and performed songs similar to "En Roulant Ma Boule." As the French settled in Canada, they brought their folk music with them and "En Roulant Ma Boule" became a favorite. Currently, over 100 versions of this well-known French-Canadian game song exist.

This arrangement opens with the **refrain,** or chorus (*a repeated section at the end of each phrase*) and is followed by a **stanza,** or verse (*a section in which the melody repeats while the words change from verse to verse*). The text tells the story of three ducks swimming in a pond, each with a special gift to offer.

Links to Learning

◆ Vocal

Read and perform the following examples in preparation for singing the opening phrase of "En Roulant Ma Boule."

◆ Theory

"En Roulant Ma Boule" is written in $\frac{6}{8}$ meter. $\frac{6}{8}$ **meter** is *a time signature in which there are two groups of three eighth notes per measure and the dotted quarter note receives the beat.* Read and perform the following example to practice reading rhythmic patterns in $\frac{6}{8}$ meter.

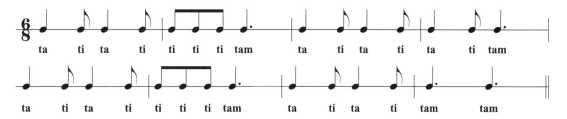

◆ Artistic Expression

To develop artistry through expressive singing, form a group of three to five singers. Ask one member of the group to observe facial expressions while the others sing the song. Identify expressions that communicate the invitation presented in the lyrics.

Evaluation

Demonstrate how well you have learned the skills and concepts featured in the lesson "En Roulant Ma Boule" by completing the following:

- Create an original story based on this song. Begin with, "Once upon a time there was a pond, and on this pond lived three ducks." Share your story with the class. In what ways can creative writing relate to singing and your performance of this song?

- Count and clap the rhythm of measures 16–24 to show your ability to read music in $\frac{6}{8}$ meter. Rate your performance on a scale of 1 to 5, with 5 being the best.

En Roulant Ma Boule

For 2-Part and Piano

Arranged by
CRISTI CARY MILLER

French Canadian Game Song

SPOTLIGHT

Posture

Posture is important for good singing. By having the body properly aligned, you are able to breathe correctly so that you have sufficient breath support needed to sing more expressively and for longer periods of time.

To experience, explore and establish proper posture for singing, try the following:

Standing

- Pretend someone is gently pulling up on a thread attached to the top of your head.

- Let out all of your air like a deflating balloon.

- Raise your arms up over your head.

- Take in a deep breath as if you were sipping through a straw.

- Slowly lower your arms down to your sides.

- Let all your air out on a breathy "pah," keeping your chest high.

- Both feet on floor, shoulder-width apart.

- Chest high, shoulders relaxed.

- Neck relaxed, head straight.

Sitting

- Sit on the edge of a chair with your feet flat on the floor while keeping your chest lifted.

- Hold your music with one hand and turn pages with the other.

- Always hold the music up so you can easily see the director and your music.

Shine On Me

Composer: Traditional Spiritual, arranged by Rollo A. Dilworth
Text: Traditional
Voicing: SSA

VOCABULARY
spiritual

arrangement

$\frac{9}{8}$ meter

simple meter

compound meter

SPOTLIGHT

To learn more about arranging, see page 53.

Focus

• Read, write and perform musical notation in compound meter.

• Relate music to history and culture.

• Perform music that represents the African American spiritual.

Getting Started

How would you define the word *light?* On the blackboard, create a list of these definitions. Since the dawning of humankind, people have used various sources of light, both natural and artificial, to fulfill their needs. Have you ever been in a strange room and found yourself reaching around with both hands, struggling to find the light switch? During slavery, African Americans found themselves in a strange land, trapped in the darkness of bondage, searching for the light—a pathway to freedom.

◆ History and Culture

"Shine On Me" is an example of an African American spiritual. **Spirituals** are *songs that are often based on biblical themes or stories and that were first sung by the slaves.* Sometimes, spirituals contain multiple or hidden meanings. In "Shine On Me," the illuminating power of light symbolizes pathways to freedom—freedom from the slavery existence, as well as freedom from the trials and tribulations of this earthly existence.

An **arrangement** is *a piece of music in which a composer takes an existing song and adds extra features or changes the song in some way.* This particular arrangement is written in a moderate swing rhythm similar to gospel music. Enjoy the lilting feel of "Shine On Me," and sing with emotion and expression.

Links to Learning

◆ Vocal

"Shine On Me" is written in $\frac{9}{8}$ **meter,** *a time signature in which there are three groups of three eighth notes per measure and the dotted quarter note receives the beat.* Perform the following example to practice reading music in $\frac{9}{8}$ meter.

do do do mi mi mi sol sol sol   mi mi mi do   do do do mi mi mi sol sol sol   mi mi mi do

◆ Theory

There are two general categories of meter: simple meter and compound meter. In **simple meter,** *the quarter note receives the beat, and the division of the beat is based on two eighth notes.* $\frac{2}{4}$, $\frac{3}{4}$ and $\frac{4}{4}$ are examples of simple meter. In **compound meter,** *the dotted quarter note receives the beat, and the division of the beat is based on three eighth notes.* $\frac{9}{8}$ meter is an example of compound meter.

Like $\frac{3}{4}$, $\frac{9}{8}$ meter is usually counted in three. Perform the following example to practice reading music in compound meter.

do   do mi   mi sol   sol mi   mi do   do do   mi mi   sol sol   mi mi   do

Now sing the example again, adding fullness to the quarter and dotted-half notes and crispness to the eighth notes.

◆ Artistic Expression

Spirituals often contain multiple or hidden meanings. Research the origin of African American spirituals. Use your findings and list ideas of what you think is meant by the line, "I wonder if the lighthouse will shine on me."

Evaluation

Demonstrate how well you have learned the skills and concepts featured in the lesson "Shine On Me" by completing the following:

- Using the pitches *do, mi,* and *sol,* write a four-measure sight-singing pattern in $\frac{9}{8}$ meter. Exchange patterns with a classmate and perform them for each other.

- In a group of four to six people, share your interpretation of the meaning of the text in "Shine On Me." What did you learn? How can a discussion on the meaning of a text improve your performance?

Commissioned by the Jubilate Children's Choir of the North Shore – Northfield, IL
Beverly Decker-Baar, Music Director

Shine On Me

For SSA and Piano

Arranged by
ROLLO A. DILWORTH

Traditional Spiritual

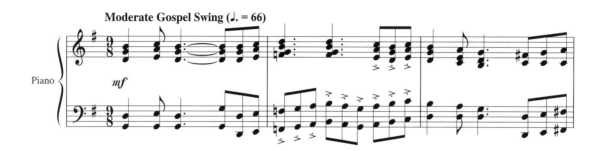

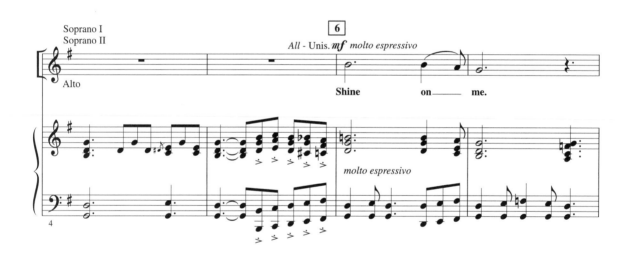

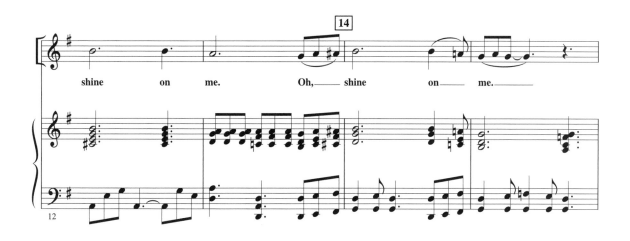

shine on me. Oh,____ shine on____ me.____

Shine on____ me. I won-der____ if the light-house____ will____

Soprano I
Unis.

Soprano II

shine on____ me._____ Shine____ on____

Alto

shine on____ me._____ Is a light

me._____ I won - der if the light - house will_____

me._____ I_____ won - der_____ if the light - house_____ will

me? I'm won-der-in', won-der-in', won-der-in' if there's a light that__ will

51

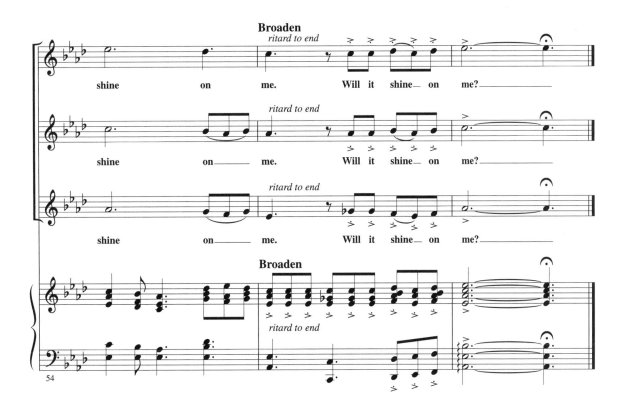

Broaden

ritard to end

shine on me. Will it shine__ on me?_____

ritard to end

shine on_____ me. Will it shine__ on me?_____

ritard to end

shine on_____ me. Will it shine__ on me?_____

Broaden

ritard to end

54

Come, Ye Sons Of Art

Composer: Henry Purcell (1659–1695), arranged by Emily Crocker
Text: attributed to Nahum Tate (1652–1715)
Voicing: 2-Part

VOCABULARY

Baroque period

ode

scale

major scale

Focus

- Describe and perform music from the Baroque period.
- Read and perform rhythmic patterns with dotted eighth and sixteenth notes.

MUSIC & HISTORY

To learn more about the Baroque period, see page 110.

Getting Started

Have you ever wondered what it would be like if someone were to write a poem or a song just for you? In fact, some songs you hear on the radio have been written in honor of or dedicated to someone special in the composer's life. For example, singer Stevie Wonder wrote the song "Isn't She Lovely" in celebration of the birth of his daughter. Elton John performs the song "Candle in the Wind" in honor of the late actress Marilyn Monroe and as a tribute to the late Princess Diana.

◆ History and Culture

During the **Baroque period** *(1600–1750)*, Western culture experienced a surge of musical life and social creativity. It was not uncommon for composers of this time to set odes to music. An **ode** is *a poem written in honor of a special person or occasion.* These poems were generally dedicated to a member of a royal family. When set to music, an ode usually includes several sections for chorus, soloists and orchestra.

English composer Henry Purcell (1659–1695) set the ode "Come, Ye Sons Of Art" to music in 1694 for Queen Mary II in honor of her birthday. Purcell was a well-known court composer and an organ maker by trade. In addition to odes, he wrote instrumental music and operas. As you sing this arrangement of "Come, Ye Sons Of Art," think about what gives the song its flair and makes it a good song for a celebration.

Links to Learning

◆ **Vocal**

This song is in the key of D major and is based on the D major scale. A **scale** is *a group of notes that are sung in succession and are based on a particular keynote or home tone.* A **major scale** is *a scale that has* "do" *as its keynote or home tone.* To locate "D" on a piano, find any set of two black keys. "D" is the white key between these two keys. This scale uses the notes D, E, F#, G, A, B, C#, D. Using the keyboard below as a guide, play the D major scale.

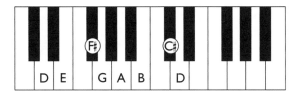

Sing the D major scale.

◆ **Theory**

Read and perform the following examples to practice clapping rhythmic patterns with dotted eighth and sixteenth notes.

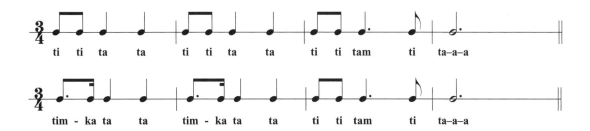

◆ **Artistic Expression**

Music of the Baroque period is elegant and has a lilting feel to it. To help you perform "Come, Ye Sons Of Art" in this style, make circles in the air and tap lightly on the palm of your hand on beat one of each measure as you sing.

Evaluation

Demonstrate how well you have learned the skills and concepts featured in the lesson "Come, Ye Sons Of Art" by completing the following:

- Discuss the musical characteristics of the Baroque period.
- Perform measures 9–21 alone or in a small group. Check for accurate rhythm and pitch.

Come, Ye Sons Of Art

For 2-Part and Piano

Edited and Arranged by
EMILY CROCKER

HENRY PURCELL
(1659–1695)

SPOTLIGHT

Pitch Matching

As you begin to learn how to read music, you must learn not only how to identify the notes on the printed page, but also how to sing the notes you read in tune. Accurate pitch matching requires that you hear the note in your head before you sing it instead of trying to find the note with your voice. Learning to sing from one note to another in scale patterns will help you hear the notes in your head before you sing them. Perform the scale below first using note names, then numbers, and finally solfège syllables.

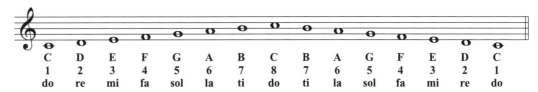

To help you sing the following examples on the correct pitch, hear the notes in your head before you sing them. If you cannot hear the interval skip in your head before you sing it, mentally sing the first note followed by all the notes in between until you come to the right note. Then, begin again and sing the pattern as written.

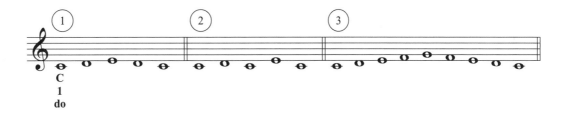

I Heard A Bird Sing

Composer: Cyndee Giebler
Text: Oliver Herford
Voicing: 2-Part

VOCABULARY

unison

minor tonality

accidental

melodic minor
  scale

$\frac{3}{4}$ meter

 SPOTLIGHT

*To learn more about
pitch matching, see
page 45.*

Focus

- Perform music in minor tonality.
- Read, write and perform rhythmic patterns in $\frac{3}{4}$ meter.

Getting Started

In a choir, there are many ways to sing. You can sing in **unison**, which means *all parts sing the same notes at the same time.* Or, you can sing a canon. In a canon, one part sings a melody, and the other parts sing the same melody but enter at different times. As you learn "I Heard A Bird Sing," you will discover that the opening and closing sections are sung in unison while the middle section is sung in a canon.

◆ History and Culture

Imagine that it is the middle of December in a cold place. The leaves have fallen from the trees. The overcast clouds have hidden the sun for days. It is dark by 4:30 p.m., leaving little time to play outdoors. This is the setting of "I Heard A Bird Sing." When it seems that winter will never end, the song of a bird reminds you that spring will soon be here.

This song is in the key of E minor and is based on the E minor scale. *A song that is based on a minor scale with* la *as its keynote, or home tone,* is described as being in **minor tonality**. The minor tonality helps to create the image of a dark and cold December day.

Links to Learning

◆ Vocal

When composing in minor tonality, it is sometimes necessary to use accidentals. An **accidental** is *a symbol used to alter or change the pitch of a note.* The most commonly used accidentals are a sharp (♯), flat (♭), or natural (♮) sign. These are used to raise, lower or return a note to its normal pitch. "I Heard A Bird Sing" is based on the E melodic minor scale. In a **melodic minor scale**, fa and sol (*the sixth and seventh pitches of the scale*) are *raised a half step to fi and si in ascending patterns, but are returned to normal when descending.* Accidentals are used to indicate these changes. Sing the E melodic minor scale.

◆ Theory

¾ **meter** is *a time signature in which there are three beats per measure and the quarter note receives the beat.* Read and perform the following rhythmic patterns in ¾ meter by clapping and chanting "beat" for each quarter note and "eighth note" for each eighth note. After you can clap and chant, step the rhythm as indicated at a slow tempo.

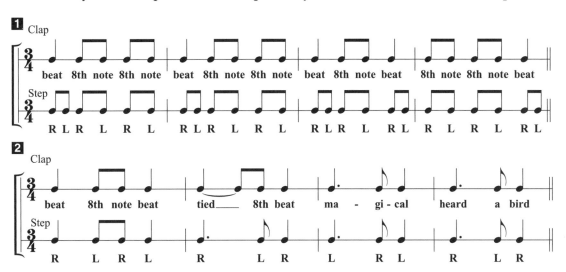

Evaluation

Demonstrate how well you have learned the skills and concepts featured in the lesson "I Heard A Bird Sing" by completing the following:

- Sing measures 5–20 alone or with others to show that you can sing on pitch in minor tonality. Evaluate how well you were able to sing in tune.

- Write a four-measure melody that is in ¾ meter and is based on the E melodic minor scale. You may want to begin and end your melody on *la* or E. Check your work for correct rhythms and pitch with a classmate.

I Heard A Bird Sing

For 2-Part and Piano

Words by
OLIVER HERFORD

Music by
CYNDEE GIEBLER

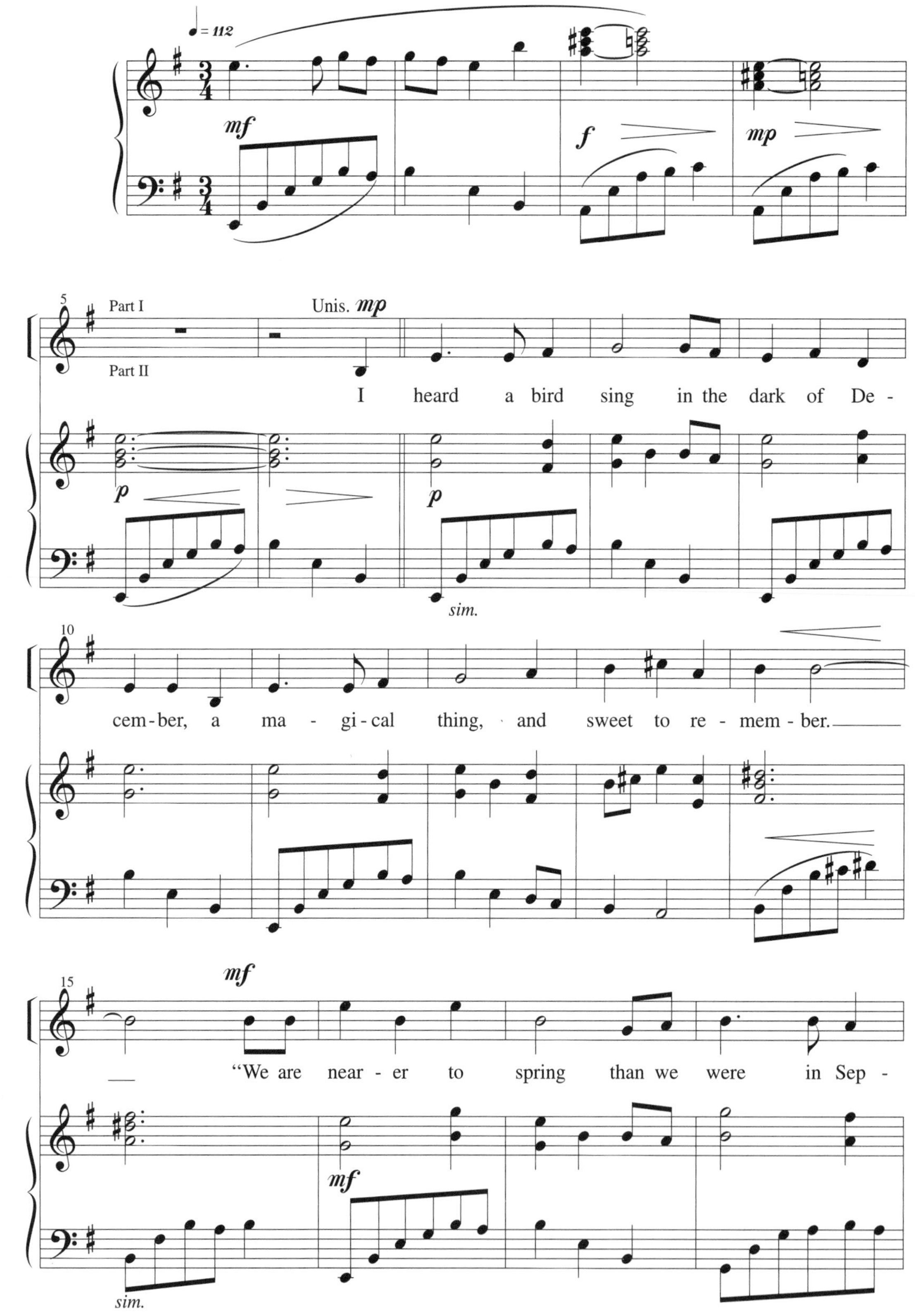

♩ = 112
mf
f
mp
5
Part I
Part II
Unis. mp
I heard a bird sing in the dark of De -
p
p
sim.
10
cem - ber, a ma - gi - cal thing, and sweet to re - mem - ber.
15
mf
"We are near - er to spring than we were in Sep -
mf
sim.

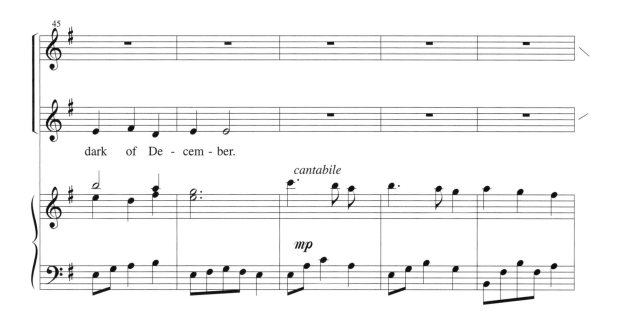

dark   of De - cem - ber.

cantabile

mp

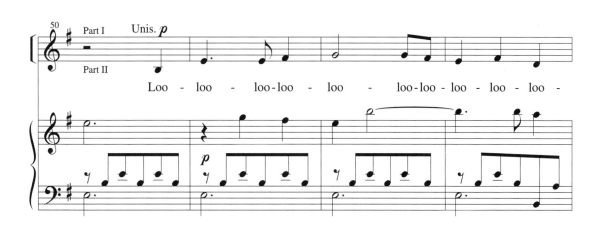

Part I   Unis. *p*

Part II

Loo - loo - loo - loo - loo   -   loo - loo - loo - loo - loo -

p

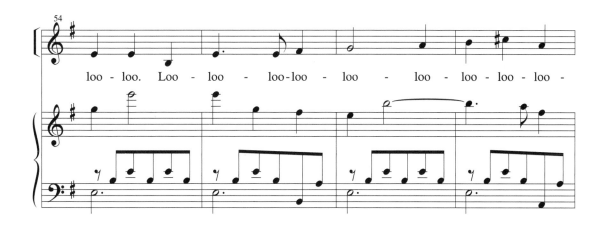

loo - loo. Loo - loo - loo - loo - loo   -   loo - loo - loo - loo -

SPOTLIGHT

Arranging

In music, an **arrangement** is *a composition in which a composer takes an existing melody and adds extra features or changes the melody in some way.* An **arranger** is *a composer who writes an arrangement by changing an existing melody to fit certain musical parameters.* The arranger has the following things to consider:

- Pitch—What is the range of the melody?
- Tempo—What is the speed of the beat?
- Instrumentation—Is the music for voices, or instruments, or both?
- Accompaniment—What will be used for accompaniment (piano, guitar, etc.), if anything?
- Harmony—What type of chords will be used for the harmony?
- Melody/Countermelody—Will harmony be added by use of a **countermelody** (*a separate vocal line that supports and contrasts the primary melody*)?

Read and perform the familiar melody "Hot Cross Buns."

Now you are ready to write your own arrangement. Using "Hot Cross Buns" as the existing melody, decide which element or elements you wish to change to compose your arrangement. You can try one or more of the ideas listed below:

- Pitch—Start the song higher or lower than currently written.
- Tempo—Alter the tempo in some manner (faster or slower).
- Instrumentation—Play the melody on different instruments.
- Accompaniment—Use a piano, guitar or other instrument to accompany your melody.
- Harmony—Add harmony notes from the chords and play them on an instrument or sing them with the melody.
- Melody/Countermelody—Compose a second melody or countermelody that fits musically with the existing melody.

Sleep, My Little One

Composer: Spanish/Mexican Lullaby, arranged by Judith Herrington and Sara Glick
Text: Traditional
Voicing: 2-Part

VOCABULARY

crescendo

decrescendo

major tonality

minor tonality

Focus

- Demonstrate how to sing phrases expressively.
- Recognize major and minor tonality through listening and singing.

 **SKILL BUILDERS**

To learn more about the keys F major and F minor, see Intermediate Sight-Singing, *pages 39–41, 76–77, 112–116 and 178–179.*

Getting Started

What is a lullaby? Name one that you know. Perhaps you are familiar with "All Through The Night" or "Hush-a-bye." What words best describe the mood you want to create when singing a lullaby? Make a list of seven descriptive words. Share your list with other members of the choir. As you perform "Sleep, My Little One," think of these descriptive words.

◆ History and Culture

"Sleep, My Little One" is a lovely lyrical lullaby that states a promise of angels who will be at the gates of heaven offering new shoes to all who arrive barefoot. This arrangement is based on the folk tune "A La Puerta del Cielo" ("At the Gate of Heaven"). Although this folk tune is attributed to Mexico, most likely it had its origins in Spain and traveled to the Americas with Spanish explorers who arrived in 1521. At that time, the best shoes were handmade specifically for the buyer. Thereby, wearing shoes implied having wealth. This was true not only in the sixteenth century, but also in ancient Egypt. Archeologists and historians have found images from around 3000 B.C. that suggest owning sandals was associated with power and wealth. "Sleep, My Little One" assures children that even if they are not wealthy enough to own shoes, angels will be at the gates of heaven to present them with new ones.

Links to Learning

◆ Vocal

Perform the following example to develop phrase shaping. Observe each **crescendo** or ————— (*a dynamic marking that indicates to gradually sing louder*) and **decrescendo** or ————— (*a dynamic marking that indicates to gradually sing softer*) to help you shape the phrase.

sol do do re mi fa re sol fa fa mi re do
loo loo loo loo loo loo loo loo loo loo loo loo loo

◆ Theory

A song that is based on a major scale with "do" as its keynote or home tone is described as being in **major tonality**. *A song that is based on a minor scale with "la" as its keynote or home tone* is described as being in **minor tonality**. Read and perform the following examples to hear the difference between major and minor tonality.

1 Major
do re mi fa sol la sol fa mi re do ti do
Minor
la ti do re mi fa mi re do ti la si la

2 Major
① ②
do do re mi do sol sol fa mi re do ti do

3 Minor
① ②
la la ti do la mi mi re do ti la si la

◆ Artistic Expression

As you sing the examples 2 and 3 above, slowly move your arm in the shape of a rainbow from left to right to outline the shape of the phrase. Then perform each example as a two-part round while continuing the arm movement.

Evaluation

Demonstrate how well you have learned the skills and concepts featured in the lesson "Sleep, My Little One" by completing the following:

- Sing measures 9–16 and outline the shape of the phrase with your arm.
- In a group of four to six singers, perform "Sleep, My Little One." Listen for and identify by measure number the major and minor sections of the song.

Composed for the Tacoma Youth Chorus, Tacoma, Washington

Sleep, My Little One
(Duermete, Niño)
For 2-Part and Piano

Vocal Arrangement by JUDITH HERRINGTON
Piano Accompaniment by SARA GLICK

Spanish/Mexican Lullaby

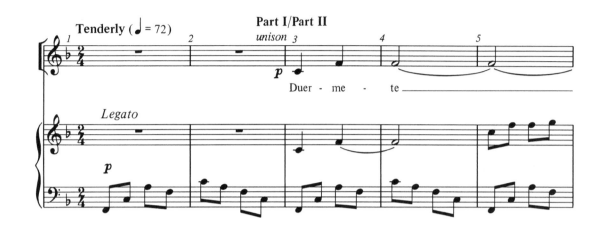

SPOTLIGHT

Breath Management

Vocal sound is produced by air flowing between the vocal cords; therefore, correct breathing is important for good singing. Good breath management provides you with the support needed to sing expressively and for longer periods of time.

To experience, explore and establish proper breathing for singing, try the following:

- Put your hands on your waist at the bottom of your rib cage.

- Take in an easy breath for four counts, as if through a straw, without lifting your chest or shoulders.

- Feel your waist and rib cage expand all the way around like an inflating inner tube.

- Let your breath out slowly on "sss," feeling your "inner tube" deflating as if it has a slow leak.

- Remember to keep your chest up the entire time.

- Take in another easy breath for four counts before your "inner tube" has completely deflated, then let your air out on "sss" for eight counts.

- Repeat this step several times, taking in an easy breath for four counts and gradually increasing the number of counts to let your air out to sixteen counts.

Sometimes in singing it is necessary to take a quick or "catch" breath.

- Look out the window and imagine seeing something wonderful for the first time, like snow.

- Point your finger at the imaginary something and let in a quick, silent breath that expresses your wonderment and surprise.

- A quick breath is not a gasping breath, but rather a silent breath.

Winter Wind

Composer: Victoria Ebel-Sabo
Text: Victoria Ebel-Sabo
Voicing: 2-Part

VOCABULARY

imitation

staggered breathing

phrase

Focus

- Perform music using staggered breathing.
- Use visual art to interpret musical imagery.

Getting Started

Which singer in your class can hold a note the longest? Take a deep breath, sing the word *wind* on any pitch, and start timing. How long was the winning time? You can make your note last longer by singing with a gentle and relaxed tone.

Sometimes a composer sets words to long, sustained notes. When the singers can successfully produce those words, the composition has a flowing and continuous line.

 SPOTLIGHT

To learn more about breath management, see page 61.

◆ History and Culture

Composer Victoria Ebel-Sabo was inspired to write "Winter Wind" after cross-country skiing in the snowy wilderness of northern Minnesota. Through her music, Ms. Ebel-Sabo describes not only what she sees, but also what she feels as she is skiing through the forest. To create this scene, she uses various musical techniques such as long, sustained notes, shifts between minor and major tonality, and **imitation**, or *the act of one part copying what another part has already played or sung.*

The composer uses music to paint a picture of the snowy forest scene. For example, she uses long notes to represent the howling of the wolf and the wind. The minor tonality captures the feeling of loneliness, and the shift to major tonality in the middle section illustrates the presence of animals in the forest. When the voice parts echo each other, they call to mind the crisscrossing animal tracks in the snow.

Links to Learning

◆ **Vocal**

Perform the following example to practice singing the word *voices* with a beautiful sustained tone on the long second syllable.

Find similar examples in "Winter Wind" that have a sustained second syllable.

Staggered breathing is *a technique that creates the overall effect of continuous singing by having each singer take a breath at different times.* Using staggered breathing, read and perform the following example with a classmate. Plan your breathing to create a continuous **phrase**, or *a musical idea with a beginning and an end.*

◆ **Artistic Expression**

Using the text of "Winter Wind," create a visual image with pencils, crayons or markers. Choose shapes and colors that represent the long and sustained tones in the music.

Evaluation

Demonstrate how well you have learned the skills and concepts featured in the lesson "Winter Wind" by completing the following:

- Select one person to serve as a listener. As a small group performs measures 19–32, have the listener decide if he or she can hear the proper use of staggered breathing.

- Share your artwork of "Winter Wind" with the class and explain how it interprets the musical imagery.

To Dan Sabo, my wilderness companion

Winter Wind

For 2-Part and Piano with Optional Oboe or Flute*

Words and Music by
VICTORIA EBEL-SABO

*Oboe or Flute part found on page 70.

Winter Wind

Oboe or Flute

VICTORIA EBEL-SABO

Concert Etiquette

The term **concert etiquette** describes *how we are expected to behave in formal musical performances.* Understanding appropriate concert etiquette allows you to be considerate of others, including audience members and performers. It also helps everyone attending to enjoy the performance.

Different types of musical performances dictate certain behavior guidelines. How one shows excitement at a rock concert is certainly worlds apart from the appropriate behavior at a formal concert or theater production. Understanding these differences allows audience members to behave in a manner that shows consideration and respect for everyone involved.

What are the expectations of a good audience member at a formal musical presentation?

- Arrive on time. If you arrive after the performance has begun, wait outside the auditorium until a break in the music to enter the hall.

- Remain quiet and still during the performance. Talking and moving around prevent others from hearing and enjoying the performance.

- Leave the auditorium only in case of an emergency. Try to leave during a break in the musical selections.

- Sing or clap along only when invited to do so by the performers or the conductor.

- Applaud at the end of a composition or when the conductor's arms are lowered at the conclusion of a performance. It is customary to not applaud between movements or sections of a major work.

- Save shouting, whistling and dancing for rock concerts or athletic events. These are never appropriate at formal musical performances.

Remembering these important behavior guidelines will ensure that everyone enjoys the show!

Non nobis Domine

Composer: William Byrd (1543–1623), edited and arranged by John Leavitt
Text: Traditional Latin
Voicing: 2-Part (Optional 3-Part), Any Combination

VOCABULARY

Renaissance period

Gregorian chant

polyphony

canon

legato

Focus

- Describe and perform music from the Renaissance period.
- Read and write rhythmic patterns with dotted quarter and eighth notes.

MUSIC & HISTORY

To learn more about the Renaissance period, see page 106.

Getting Started

Imagine you are in a large city at an outdoor marketplace. You see a great throng of people approaching. Many of the people are heading toward an outdoor stage where a new play by William Shakespeare is about to begin. A choir, under the direction of composer William Byrd, is rehearsing a brand new piece in the nearby cathedral. Where and when is all of this taking place? You are in England during the late sixteenth century.

◆ History and Culture

William Byrd (1543–1623), often considered the "father of British music," lived in England during the late **Renaissance period** *(1430–1600)*. He was appointed Organist and Master of the Choristers at the Lincoln Cathedral when he was only nineteen years old. He was a performer and composer of music for both voice and the keyboard.

In the years prior to the Renaissance period, a significant sacred musical form was the **Gregorian chant**, or *a single unaccompanied melodic line sung by male voices*. As this style developed, additional melodic lines were added. This was the beginning of **polyphony**, or *a type of music in which two or more different melodic lines are sung at the same time*. Polyphonic music was refined during the Renaissance, and this period is sometimes called the "golden age of polyphony."â "Non nobis Domine" is a good example of early polyphony.

Links to Learning

◆ Theory

Clap the following example to feel the rhythmic flow of each line. Then, step the rhythms while speaking each word.

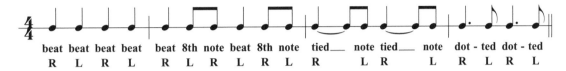

"Non nobis Domine" is a **canon**, or *a form of music where one part sings a melody and the other parts sing the same melody, entering a short time after the first part has begun.* With a partner, clap the following example as a canon. Make a "palms up" motion for each rest. Begin at the first measure, and have your partner begin when you reach the second measure. Repeat the example and step the rhythms while speaking each word. Remain still during the rest, and feel its full duration.

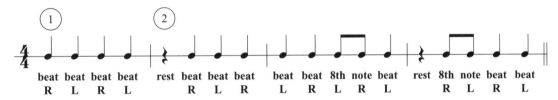

◆ Artistic Expression

Although the rhythmic patterns in "Non nobis Domine" have a steady pulse, the melodic line is **legato**, or *a connected and sustained style of singing.* Look at measures 1–10 in the music. Identify the three long phrases in this section. As you sing, use a scarf and make a long, graceful arc over your head, outlining the shape of each phrase.

Evaluation

Demonstrate how well you have learned the skills and concepts featured in the lesson "Non nobis Domine" by completing the following:

- Discuss the musical characteristics of the Renaissance period.

- Compose your own four-measure rhythmic pattern using both dotted rhythms and rests. Play your composition on a rhythm instrument for the class. Was your rhythm notation correct? Were you able to perform the pattern accurately?

Non nobis Domine

For 2-Part/3-Part, Any Combination, a cappella

Edited and Arranged by
JOHN LEAVITT

Traditional Latin Text
Music by
WILLIAM BYRD (1543–1623)

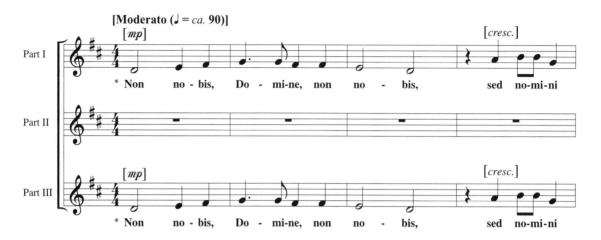

Part I: * Non no-bis, Do-mi-ne, non no-bis, sed no-mi-ni

Part II:

Part III: * Non no-bis, Do-mi-ne, non no-bis, sed no-mi-ni

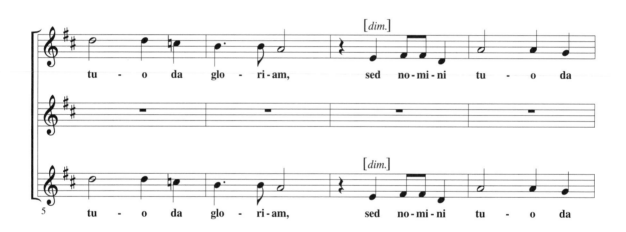

tu - o da glo-ri-am, sed no-mi-ni tu - o da

tu - o da glo-ri-am, sed no-mi-ni tu - o da

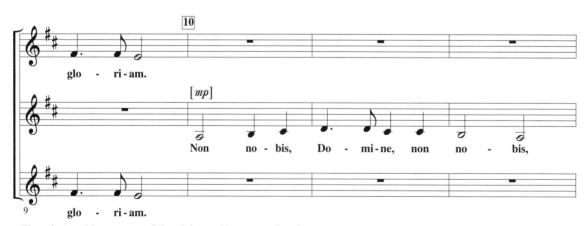

glo - ri-am.

Non no-bis, Do - mi-ne, non no - bis,

glo - ri-am.

*Translation: Not unto us, O Lord, but to Your name be glory given.

SPOTLIGHT

Careers In Music

Teacher

Music teachers share their love of music with their students. To become a public school teacher, you must have a bachelor's degree in music education. That will require at least four years of college, including one semester of student teaching. High school and junior high music teachers usually specialize in one performance area such as choir, band or orchestra. They may also teach general music, music theory, music appreciation, keyboard and guitar. Elementary music teachers enjoy working with young children. Their job is varied in that they teach singing, dancing, how to play instruments, listening, world music and much more.

At the college level, a music professor must have additional training. Although the minimum requirement is to have a master's degree in music, most colleges require you to have a doctorate as well. College professors teach students how to become professional musicians and professional teachers.

Some musicians choose to teach music through their church or synagogue. Church musicians may be full-time or part-time employees. They might serve as a singer, a choir director, an organist, an instrumentalist or a **cantor** *(a person who sings and teaches music in temples or synagogues).* Some of these positions require a college degree in music.

Private studio teachers enjoy working with students on a one-on-one basis. They teach from their homes, from a private studio, or sometimes at a school. Private instructors teach voice, piano/keyboard, or any of the musical instruments. Their hours are flexible, but they often work in the evenings or weekends because that is when their students are not in school.

Das Blümchen Wunderhold

Composer: Ludwig van Beethoven (1770–1827), arranged by Emily Crocker
Text: Gottfried August Bürger (1747–1794), English text by Emily Crocker
Voicing: Unison Voices/2-Part

VOCABULARY

lyrics

Classical period

symphony

art song

articulation

Focus

• Describe and perform music from the Classical period.

• Sing musical phrases that are clean and clear in character.

• Relate music to other subjects.

To learn more about the Classical period, see page 114.

Getting Started

One feature of choral music that makes it special is the use of **lyrics**, or *the words to a song.* As singers, it is important that your words are understood so you can communicate a song's meaning to your audience. "Das Blümchen Wunderhold," or "The Loveliest Flower," was originally written in German, but it has been translated into English. Before learning the notes and rhythms, read through the text. In your own words, give a summary of the song's meaning. This will help you better communicate the words of "Das Blümchen Wunderhold" to your audience.

◆ History and Culture

Ludwig van Beethoven (1770–1827) is regarded as one of the greatest composers of all time. Born in Bonn, Germany, he lived during the late **Classical period** *(1750–1820)*. He came from a family of musicians, and his first piece of music was published when he was twelve. Among his many works, Beethoven wrote nine **symphonies** *(large-scale works for orchestra with separate contrasting sections).* He also composed music for solo piano and ensemble music for other instruments. Beethoven's music spans over two periods of music history. His earlier works, such as "Das Blümchen Wunderhold" are considered Classical, whereas his later works are often classified as Romantic.

As for his vocal music, Beethoven composed large works for chorus and orchestra, and in contrast, he wrote smaller pieces for solo voice and piano. "Das Blümchen Wunderhold" is an example of this. Published in 1805, it is an **art song**, or *a musical setting of a poem for solo voice and piano accompaniment.* The song's text compares the beauty of a tiny flower to love between two people. Enjoy learning this pretty song.

Links to Learning

◆ Vocal

Music from the Classical period features melodic lines that are clean and clear in character. **Articulation**, *the amount of separation or connection between notes*, contributes to the clarity of the melodic line. Perform the following examples to practice styles of articulation found in Classical music.

◆ Artistic Expression

Singers often use visual images to enhance their performance. Think about the type of flower described in this song. Is it a rose, a daffodil or an orchid? Draw or find a picture of your choice for "The Loveliest Flower" and share it with the class.

Evaluation

Demonstrate how well you have learned the skills and concepts featured in the lesson "Das Blümchen Wunderhold" by completing the following:

• Discuss the musical characteristics of the Classical period.

• Alone or in a small group, sing the first verse of this song to show that you can sing phrases that are clean and clear in character. How did you do?

• In your own words, write out a summary of the meaning of the text of this song. Share you work with a classmate and compare your interpretations. How are they similar? How are they different?

Das Blümchen Wunderhold
(The Loveliest Flower)

Arranged with English Text by
EMILY CROCKER

LUDWIG VAN BEETHOVEN
(1770–1827)

SPOTLIGHT

Changing Voice

As we grow in size and maturity, we don't always grow at the same rate. Just look around your school or neighborhood. Some thirteen-year-olds tower over others, while some are quite small.

As the voice matures, it changes in both pitch and **timbre** *(tone quality).* Just like growing in stature, this process is not the same for every person. One person's voice might drop an octave almost overnight, while another person's might not seem to have changed at all.

The Male Voice

As a young male singer, you will face several challenges as your voice matures. Certain pitches that were once easy to sing suddenly may be out of your vocal range. While every voice change is unique, many male singers progress through several identifiable stages:

1. The voice is a treble voice with no obvious signs of changing.

2. The upper range sounds slightly breathy or hoarse.

3. The singer is able to sing lower pitches than before. Higher pitches continue to sound breathy. The speaking and singing voices are noticeably lower. There is an obvious "break" around middle C.

4. The voice "settles" into **Bass** *(the lowest-sounding male voice)* or "rises" to **Tenor** *(the highest-sounding male voice).* Higher pitches can now be sung in **falsetto,** *a register in the male voice that extends far above the natural high voice.*

With practice and attention to the principles of good singing, you can get through this transition without too much difficulty.

The Female Voice

As a young female singer, you will not face the same challenges that young male singers face. However, your voice will go through changes, too.

Between the ages of eleven and sixteen, you might notice breathiness in your vocal tone, difficulty in moving between your chest voice and head voice, and a general lack of vocal resonance.

By using the good vocal techniques of posture, breath and vowel formation, you can establish all the qualities necessary for success. You should use your full vocal range and gain experience in singing both **Alto** *(the lowest-sounding female voice)* and **Soprano** *(the highest-sounding female voice),* since your actual voice category may not be evident until you reach your middle-to-late teens.

Pie Jesu

Composer: Gabriel Fauré (1845–1924), arranged by John Leavitt
Text: Traditional Latin
Voicing: Unison Voices

VOCABULARY

Romantic period

requiem

intonation

phrase

MUSIC&HISTORY

To learn more about the Romantic period, see page 118.

Focus

- Describe and perform music from the Romantic period.
- Sing phrases expressively.

Getting Started

One reason that music is found in every corner of the world is that it often connects with human emotions. How do you feel when you hear "The Star Spangled Banner," "Amazing Grace," or the "Theme From *Jaws*"? Write these words on the board: *excitement, sadness,* and *anger.* Beneath each word, list titles of songs that can bring out these emotions. Every time you rehearse "Pie Jesu" with its simple beauty, think of the emotions this piece brings out in you.

◆ History and Culture

French composer Gabriel Fauré (1845–1924) is often regarded as the greatest master of French song. He lived during the **Romantic period** *(1820–1900).* His music features soaring melodic lines and complex harmonies; both of these are characteristics of the period. He was a church organist and also a professor of composition at the Paris Conservatory.

Primarily a composer of smaller works, Fauré wrote music for both instruments and voice. However, he did write a few larger pieces, including his famous *Requiem.* A **requiem,** or *mass for the dead,* seeks to honor the dead and comfort the living. The Latin word *requiem* can be translated as "rest." "Pie Jesu," a section of the *Requiem,* is a request made by the living on behalf of the dead for eternal peace and rest.

Links to Learning

◆ Vocal

"Pie Jesu" is in the key of G major and is based on the G major scale. To locate "G" on a piano, find any set of three black keys. "G" is the white key to the left of the middle black key. This scale uses the notes G, A, B, C, D, E, F♯, G. Using the keyboard below as a guide, play the G major scale.

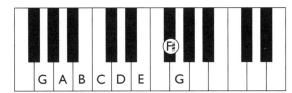

Sing the G major scale.

Read and perform the following example as you prepare to sing "Pie Jesu." Sing in a connected and sustained style, and pay close attention to your **intonation**, or *in-tune singing.*

◆ Artistic Expression

A **phrase** is *a musical idea with a beginning and an end.* Sing the phrase in measures 11–16 of "Pie Jesu" while drawing an arch in the air above your head. Shape your phrase by beginning softly at measure 11. Your phrase should be loudest at the highest point of your arch and softest at its lowest point. Notice the various dynamic markings in the music and use these as a guide for shaping your phrase.

Evaluation

Demonstrate how well you have learned the skills and concepts featured in the lesson "Pie Jesu" by completing the following:

- Discuss the musical characteristics of the Romantic period.

- Study measures 19–24 to decide on a phrase shape for this section based on the melodic line and dynamics. Alone or in a small group, sing the measures and show your understanding of phrasing. How did you do?

Pie Jesu
from *Requiem*

For Unison Voices and Piano

Arranged by
JOHN LEAVITT

GABRIEL FAURÉ
(1845–1924)

SPOTLIGHT

Vocal Jazz

Jazz is *an original American style of music that features improvisation, syncopation and swing rhythms.* Although jazz is largely an instrumental expression, vocal jazz holds a prominent position in the genre. Ella Fitzgerald (1917–1996), called the "First Lady of Song," was one of the most famous vocal jazz singers of the twentieth century. Through her career, Ella won thirteen Grammy awards with her amazing talent and flexible voice. She was a master at **improvisation** (*the art of singing music, making it up as you go*) and **scat singing** (*an improvisational style of singing that uses nonsense syllables instead of words*).

Jazz, and more specifically vocal jazz, has distinctive rhythmic and melodic performance characteristics. **Swing rhythms,** or *rhythms in which the second eighth note of each beat is played or sung like the last third of a triplet, creating an uneven "swing" feel,* are common in jazz. The following melodic characteristics or inflections are described in the book *Vocal Jazz Style,* written by composer and vocal jazz artist Dr. Kirby Shaw.

Accent

Sing the note with extra
emphasis or stress.

Ascending Smear

Slide into the note from
one half step below.

Legato

Sing notes in a connected
and sustained style.

Fall-off

Sing a descending slide followed
by a rest, similar to a sigh.

Staccato

Sing notes in a short
and detached style.

Glissando

Sing an upward slide
between two pitches.

You can have fun with these vocal jazz techniques. Think of a simple familiar song. Apply some of these techniques as you sing the song. One of Ella Fitzgerald's first hits was "A-Tisket, A-Tasket," sung in an improvisational jazz style. You can be a jazz singer, too!

Can you count the stars?

Composer: Jonathan Willcocks (b. 1953)
Text: Johann Hey (1789–1854), translated by H. W. Dulcken
Voicing: 2-Part

VOCABULARY

Contemporary period

mixed meter

skip-wise motion

duet

MUSIC & HISTORY

To learn more about the Contemporary period, see page 122.

Focus

- Describe and perform music from the Contemporary period.
- Read, write and perform music in mixed meter.

Getting Started

Imagine being outside on a clear, dark night in a place where there are no streetlights or moon to hide the wonders in the sky. Only on a night like this do we realize how many stars are in the heavens! Would you be able to count them? Just trying would make you dizzy. In "Can you count the stars?" the writer compares the number of stars with the number of children on the earth.

◆ History and Culture

"Can you count the stars?" is a musical composition from the **Contemporary period** (*1900–present*). One common practice in this period is to compose music in **mixed meter**, *a technique in which the time signature frequently changes within a piece.* Look at the music. How many different time signatures can you find?

In this song, British composer Jonathan Willcocks (b. 1953) has set to music a poem about the number of stars in the universe. You will sing about twinkling stars, floating clouds, and the sweet voices of happy children. Notice how Willcocks paints a musical picture describing the various aspects of the poem.

Links to Learning

◆ Vocal

Skip-wise motion is *the movement from a given note to another note that is two or more notes above or below it on the staff.* Read and perform the following examples to practice singing in skip-wise motion. "Can you count the stars?" contains many of these skips.

◆ Theory

"Can you count the stars?" is written in mixed meter. Perform the following examples to practice reading and clapping rhythmic patterns in mixed meter. Keep the eighth note constant and the beat steady.

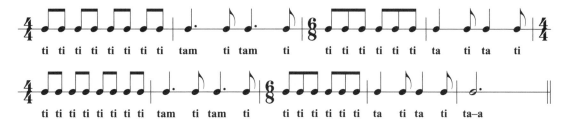

Evaluation

Demonstrate how well you have learned the skills and concepts featured in the lesson "Can you count the stars?" by completing the following:

- Discuss the musical characteristics of the Contemporary period.

- As a **duet** (*two singers*), perform measures 54–57 with one person on each part to show that you can sing music with skip-wise motion accurately. How did you do?

- Using the rhythmic patterns found in the Theory section above as a guide, create your own four-measure pattern in mixed meter. Check your work for correct rhythms in each meter.

Can you count the stars?

For 2-Part and Piano

Words by JOHANN HEY (1789–1854)
Translated by H.W. DULCKEN

Music by
JONATHAN WILLCOCKS

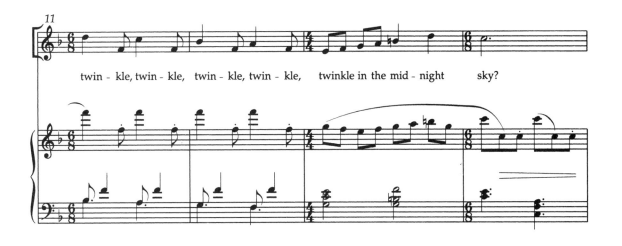

twin - kle, twin - kle, twin - kle, twin - kle, twinkle in the mid - night sky?

Can you count the

clouds, _____ count the clouds, so light - ly float-ing

light - ly, light - ly, light - ly, light - ly o'er the meadows float - ing by?

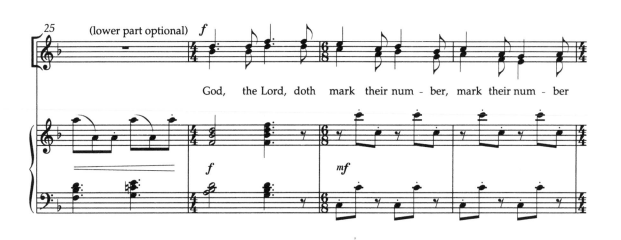

(lower part optional)

God, the Lord, doth mark their num - ber, mark their num - ber

With his eyes that ne - ver slum - ber, ne - ver slum - ber; He hath

o'er the meadows float - ing by?

God, the Lord, doth

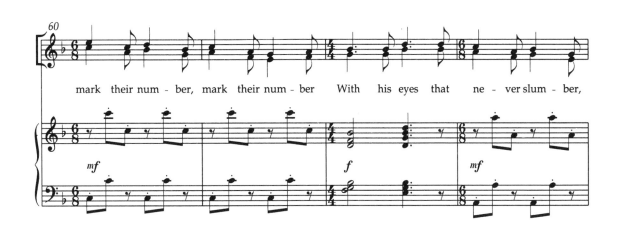

mark their num - ber, mark their num - ber   With his eyes that ne - ver slum - ber,

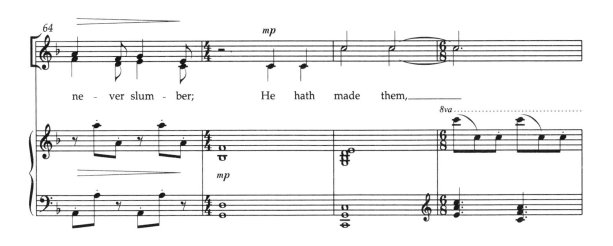

ne - ver slum - ber;   He hath made them,_____

chil - dren rise each morn- ing, rise each morn- ing, rise eachmorning blithe and

gay?

(*mf*)

Canyou count their jolly

voi - ces, _____ can you count their jolly voi - - ces, _

loves them, _____ and he

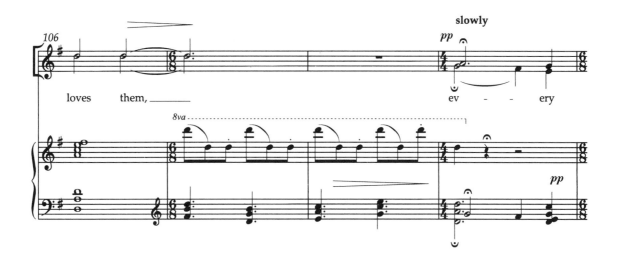

loves them, _____ ev - ery

one.

Improvisation

Improvisation is *the art of singing or playing music, making it up as you go.* **Scat singing** is *an improvisational style of singing that uses nonsense syllables instead of words.* Sometimes, these nonsense sounds can imitate the sound of an instrument. Scat singing, especially as a solo, can be the scariest part of singing jazz.

Dr. Kirby Shaw, one of the top vocal jazz composers and conductors in the world today, offers some suggestions to help build your confidence in this fun and exciting art form.

Start your scat solo with a short melodic or rhythmic idea from the tune being performed. There is nothing wrong with having a preconceived idea before starting to sing a scat solo! By gradually developing the idea as you sing, you will have an organized solo that sounds completely improvised.

Start with scat syllables like "doo" when singing swing tunes. Try "bee," "dee" and "dn" for an occasional accented eighth note on the *and* of beats (1 *and* 2 *and* 3 *and* 4 *and*). Try "doot" or "dit" for short last notes of musical phrases.

Be able to imitate any sound you like from the world around you, such as a soft breeze, a car horn or a musical instrument. There might be a place for that sound in one of your solos.

Listen to and imitate, note-for-note, the great jazz singers and instrumentalists. You can be inspired by musicians like Ella Fitzgerald, Jon Hendricks, Louis Armstrong or Charlie Parker.

Learn to sing the blues. You can listen to artists like B. B. King, Stevie Ray Vaughan, Buddy Guy or Luther Allison. There are many types of recordings from which to choose.

In short, learn as many different kinds of songs as you can. The best scat singers quote from such diverse sources as nursery rhymes, African chant and even opera. Above all, have fun as you develop your skills!

Music & History

Links to Music

 Sandro Botticelli (1445–1510) was an Italian painter who lived and worked in Florence, Italy, during the Renaissance. *The Adoration of the Magi* reflects the Renaissance interest in religious subjects. Framing the central figures within the strong geometric pillars emphasized those figures over others. Botticelli was also commissioned by the Pope to paint frescoes in the Sistine Chapel in the Vatican.

Sandro Botticelli. *The Adoration of the Magi.* c. 1480. Tempera and oil on panel. 70.2 x 104.2 cm (27 5/8 x 41"). National Gallery of Art, Washington, D. C. Andrew W. Mellon Collection.

Focus

- Describe the Renaissance period, including important developments.
- Describe characteristics of Renaissance music.

The Renaissance— A Time of Exploration

The **Renaissance period** *(1430–1600)* was a time during the fifteenth and sixteenth centuries of rapid development in exploration, science, art and music. This period could be called the beginning of modern history and the beginning of Western civilization as we know it now.

The development and use of the compass as a navigational aid in China made it possible for explorers to travel to new continents and to discover other cultures. Renaissance sailors first took to the seas to supply Europeans with Asian spices such as peppercorns, nutmeg and cinnamon. Also from the East came precious jewels and fine silk, a fabric especially valued for women's clothing.

Sailors also brought back information and customs from other cultures. This new information, along with a revived interest in writings from the ancient Greek and Roman cultures, was quickly spread across Europe, thanks to the invention of the printing press and mass-produced books. The invention of the printing press, credited to Johann Gutenberg, was one of the most significant developments of the Renaissance. As books became more available and less expensive, more people learned to read and began to consider new ideas.

A major change in the Christian religion occurred at this time. During the Protestant Reformation, various groups of Christians left the Catholic Church and formed some of the present-day Protestant denominations. Many Protestant groups translated Bibles from the Catholic Church's language of Latin to the language spoken by the people.

Remarkable advances were made in the arts and sciences by:

- Thomas Weelkes—English composer
- Gerardus Mercator—German mapmaker
- Vasco da Gama—Portuguese explorer who rounded the Horn of Africa and went on to India

COMPOSERS

Josquin des Prez
(c. 1450–1521)

Andrea Gabrieli
(c. 1510–1586)

Michael Praetorius
(1571–1621)

Thomas Weelkes
(c. 1576–1623)

ARTISTS

Gentile Bellini
(1429–1507)

Sandro Botticelli
(1445–1510)

Leonardo da Vinci
(1452–1519)

Michelangelo
(1475–1564)

Raphael
(1483–1520)

AUTHORS

Martin Luther
(1483–1546)

William Shakespeare
(1565–1616)

VOCABULARY

Renaissance period

sacred music

mass

motet

secular music

lute

polyphony

a cappella

madrigal

word painting

Renaissance Music

During the Renaissance, the Catholic Church gradually lost some of its influence over the daily lives of people. Much of the important music of the period, however, was still **sacred music**, or *music associated with religious services and themes*. In music, a **mass** is *a religious service of prayers and ceremonies*. A **motet** is *a shorter choral work, also set to a Latin text and used in religious services, but not part of the regular mass*. These two types of compositions were the most important forms of sacred Renaissance music. In Protestant churches, sacred music was composed and sung in the languages of the worshippers.

Like sacred music, **secular music**, or *music not associated with religious services or themes*, flourished during the Renaissance period. The center of musical activity gradually began to shift from churches to castles and towns. Music became an important form of entertainment for members of the emerging middle class. Social dancing became more widespread. Dance music of this period was written for **lute**, *an early form of the guitar*, and other instruments.

The Renaissance period is often referred to as the "golden age of polyphony." **Polyphony**, which literally means "many-sounding," is *a type of music in which there are two or more different melodic lines being sung or played at the same time*. Much of the choral music of the time was polyphonic, with as many as sixteen different vocal parts. Instruments were sometimes used to accompany and echo the voices.

Performance Links

When performing music of the Renaissance period, it is important to apply the following guidelines:

- Sing with clarity and purity of tone.
- Balance the vocal lines with equal importance.
- In polyphonic music, sing the rhythms accurately and with precision.
- When designated by the composer, sing **a cappella** *(unaccompanied or without instruments)*.

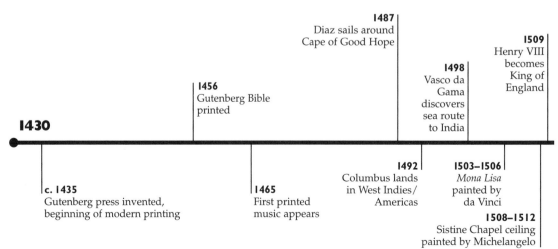

Listening Links

CHORAL SELECTION

"As Vesta Was Descending" by Thomas Weelkes (c.1576–1623)

Thomas Weelkes was an important English composer and organist. "As Vesta Was Descending" is an outstanding example of a **madrigal**, *a musical setting of a poem in three or more parts*. Generally, a madrigal has a secular text and is sung a cappella. This madrigal was written in honor of Queen Elizabeth I of England. This piece is an excellent example of **word painting**, *a technique in which the music reflects the meaning of the words*. Listen carefully to discover what occurs in the music on the following words: "descending," "ascending," "running down amain," "two by two," "three by three," and "all alone." Why do you think Weelkes chose to use the repeated text at the end?

INSTRUMENTAL SELECTION

"Three Voltas" from *Terpsichore* by Michael Praetorius (1571–1621)

During the Renaissance, a favorite type of composition involved a combination of dances in changing tempos and meters. Some of the dance music developed into stylized pieces for listening, which were not intended for actual dancing. *Terpsichore*, by German composer Michael Praetorius, is a collection of 312 short dance pieces, written in four, five or six parts, with no particular instrumentation specified.

You will hear authentic early instruments in this recording. By listening carefully, guess which modern-day instruments are descended from these early ones.

Check Your Understanding

1. List three major nonmusical changes that took place during the Renaissance period.
2. Describe polyphony as heard in "As Vesta Was Descending."
3. Describe how music from the Renaissance is different from music of today.

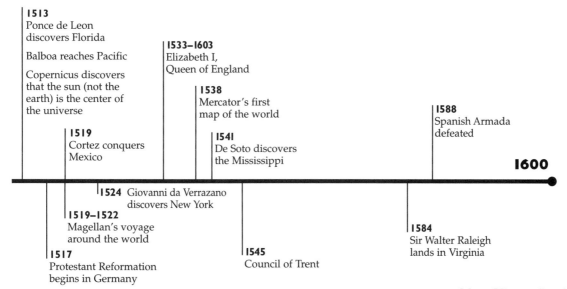

1513
Ponce de Leon
discovers Florida

Balboa reaches Pacific

Copernicus discovers
that the sun (not the
earth) is the center of
the universe

1519
Cortez conquers
Mexico

1533–1603
Elizabeth I,
Queen of England

1538
Mercator's first
map of the world

1541
De Soto discovers
the Mississippi

1588
Spanish Armada
defeated

1600

1524 Giovanni da Verrazano
discovers New York

1519–1522
Magellan's voyage
around the world

1517
Protestant Reformation
begins in Germany

1545
Council of Trent

1584
Sir Walter Raleigh
lands in Virginia

 The work of the Italian painter Orazio Gentileschi (1563–1639) was influenced by the innovative style of Caravaggio. In later years, Orazio's works tend to place a single figure or a restricted figure group in sharp relief before a dark background. The subject of this painting, St. Cecilia, is often referred to as the patron saint of music. She is playing a small table pipe organ.

Orazio Gentileschi. *Saint Cecilia and an Angel*. c. 1610. Oil on canvas. 87.8 x 108.1 cm (34 5/8 x 42 1/2"). National Gallery of Art, Washington, D. C. Samuel H. Kress Collection.

Focus
- Describe the Baroque period, including important developments.
- Describe characteristics of Baroque music.

The Baroque Period— A Time of Elaboration

The **Baroque period** *(1600–1750)* was a time of powerful kings and their courts. In Europe, elaborate clothing, hats and hairstyles for the wealthy men and women matched the decorated buildings, gardens, furniture and paintings of this period. The term *baroque* comes from a French word for "imperfect or irregular pearls." Often, pearls were used as decorations on clothing.

There was a great interest in science and exploration. During the Baroque period, Galileo perfected the telescope by 1610, providing the means for greater exploration of the universe. Sir Isaac Newton identified gravity and formulated principles of physics and mathematics. Bartolomeo Cristofori developed the modern pianoforte in which hammers strike the strings. Exploration of new worlds continued, and colonization of places discovered during the Renaissance increased.

Most paintings and sculptures of the time were characterized by their large scale and dramatic details. Artwork celebrated the splendor of royal rulers. For example, the Palace at Versailles near Paris, was built and decorated as a magnificent setting for King Louis XIV of France. It features notably elaborate architecture, paintings, sculptures and gardens.

The Baroque period was a time of great changes brought about through the work of extraordinary people such as:

- Johann Sebastian Bach—German composer
- Orazio Gentileschi—Italian painter
- Alexander Pope—English poet
- Galileo Galilei—Italian mathematician who used his new telescope to prove that the Milky Way is made up of individual stars

COMPOSERS
Johann Pachelbel
(1653–1706)

Antonio Vivaldi
(1678–1741)

Johann Sebastian Bach
(1685–1750)

George Frideric Handel
(1685–1759)

ARTISTS
El Greco
(1541–1614)

Orazio Gentileschi
(1563–1639)

Peter Paul Rubens
(1577–1640)

Rembrandt van Rijn
(1606–1669)

Jan Steen
(1626–1679)

Jan Vermeer
(1632–1675)

AUTHORS
Ben Jonson
(1572–1637)

René Descartes
(1596–1650)

John Milton
(1608–1674)

Molière
(1622–1673)

Alexander Pope
(1688–1744)

Samuel Johnson
(1709–1784)

VOCABULARY
Baroque period

basso continuo

opera

oratorio

concerto grosso

Baroque Music

The music of the Baroque period shows the same kind of dramatic flair that characterized the clothing, architecture and art of the time. Most of the compositions of that period have a strong sense of movement, often including a **basso continuo**, or *a continually moving bass line.*

The Baroque period brought about a great interest in instrumental music. Keyboard instruments were refined, including the clavichord, harpsichord and organ. The modern string family of instruments were now used, and the trumpet became a favorite melody instrument in orchestras.

During the Baroque period, a number of new forms of music were developed. **Opera**, *a combination of singing, instrumental music, dancing and drama that tells a story,* was created beginning with *Orfeo*, by Claudio Monteverdi (1567–1643). The **oratorio**, *a large-scale work for solo voices, chorus and orchestra based on a literary or religious theme,* was also developed. In 1741, George Frideric Handel (1685–1759) composed the *Messiah*, one of the most famous oratorios still performed today. The **concerto grosso** *(a multi-movement Baroque piece for a group of soloists and an orchestra)* was also made popular with Antonio Vivaldi's (1678–1741) *The Four Seasons* and Johann Sebastian Bach's (1685–1750) *Brandenberg Concertos.*

Performance Links

When performing music of the Baroque period, it is important to apply the following guidelines:

- Sing with accurate pitch.
- Be conscious of who has the dominant theme and make sure the accompanying part or parts do not overshadow the melody.
- Keep a steady, unrelenting pulse in most pieces. Precision of dotted rhythms is especially important.
- When dynamic level changes occur, all vocal lines need to change together.

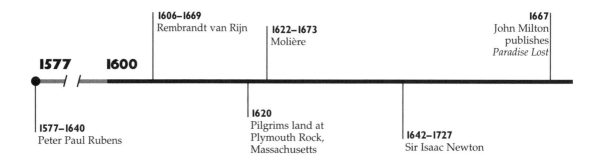

Listening Links

CHORAL SELECTION

"Gloria in excelsis Deo" from *Gloria in D Major* by Antonio Vivaldi (1678–1741)

Antonio Vivaldi was one of the greatest composers and violinists of his time. He wrote operas and concertos, as well as sacred works (oratorios, motets and masses) for chorus, soloists and orchestra. One of his most popular choral works is the *Gloria in D Major* mass. "Gloria in excelsis Deo" is a magnificent choral piece. It is full of energy and emotion that is expressed with great drama. It was composed for three solo voices and chorus, and is accompanied by a variety of instruments. Does ornamentation occur in the vocal parts, in the accompaniment, or both?

INSTRUMENTAL SELECTION

"The Arrival of the Queen of Sheba" from *Solomon* by George Frideric Handel (1685–1759)

George Frideric Handel was a German-born composer who lived in England for most of his life. The oratorio *Solomon* tells the story of King Solomon, of tenth-century Israel. Solomon was known for his great wisdom. Sheba, the Queen of Ethiopia, came to visit and challenge Solomon, but he wisely answered all her questions, and she left as an ally. *Solomon* was written for two choruses, five soloists, a chamber orchestra and a harpsichord. Two instruments are featured playing a duet in this piece. What is the name of these instruments, and to what instrument family do they belong?

Check Your Understanding

1. List three major nonmusical developments that took place during the Baroque period.

2. How would the performance of the oratorio *Solomon* differ from the performance of an opera?

3. Describe how music from the Baroque period is different from music of the Renaissance.

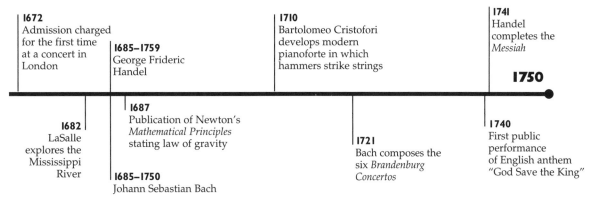

1672
Admission charged for the first time at a concert in London

1685–1759
George Frideric Handel

1710
Bartolomeo Cristofori develops modern pianoforte in which hammers strike strings

1741
Handel completes the *Messiah*

1750

1682
LaSalle explores the Mississippi River

1687
Publication of Newton's *Mathematical Principles* stating law of gravity

1685–1750
Johann Sebastian Bach

1721
Bach composes the six *Brandenburg Concertos*

1740
First public performance of English anthem "God Save the King"

French artist Elisabeth Vigée-LeBrun (1755–1842) lived and worked in Paris during the time of the French Revolution and was forced to flee the city in disguise in 1789. A majority of Vigeé-LeBrun paintings are portraits of women and children. This painting expresses friendship and maternal love.

Elisabeth Vigée-LeBrun. *The Marquise de Pezé and the Marquise de Rouget with Her Two Children.* 1787. Oil on canvas. 123.4 x 155.9 cm (48 5/8 x 61 3/8"). National Gallery of Art, Washington, D. C. Gift of the Bay Foundation in memory of Josephine Bay and Ambassador Charles Ulrick Bay.

Focus

- Describe the Classical period, including important developments.
- Describe characteristics of Classical music.

The Classical Period— A Time of Balance, Clarity and Simplicity

The **Classical period** *(1750–1820)* was a time when people became influenced by the early Greeks and Romans for examples of order and ways of living life. Travelers of the period visited the ruins of ancient Egypt, Rome and Greece and brought the ideas of the ancients to the art and architecture of the time. As a result, the calm beauty and simplicity of this classical art from the past inspired artists and musicians to move away from the overly decorated styles of the Baroque period. The music, art and architecture reflected a new emphasis on emotional restraint and simplicity.

In the intellectual world, there was increasing emphasis on individual reason and enlightenment. Writers such as Voltaire and Thomas Jefferson suggested that through science and democracy, rather than mystery and monarchy, people could choose their own fate. Such thinking, brought on by the enlarging middle class and the excesses of the wealthy royal class, was the beginning of important political changes in society. In many parts of Europe, the power and authority of royalty were attacked, and members of the middle class struggled for their rights. There was a revolution against England by the American colonies, which resulted in the establishment of the United States. In France, the monarchy was overthrown, and the king and most of his court were beheaded.

Some of the most important contributors of the time were:

- Wolfgang Amadeus Mozart—Austrian composer
- Elisabeth Vigée-Lebrun—French painter
- Ben Franklin—American writer, inventor, diplomat
- Joseph Priestley—English chemist who discovered oxygen
- Robert Fulton—American inventor who produced the first submarine, "Nautilus"

COMPOSERS

Carl Philipp Emanuel Bach
(1714–1788)

Johann Christian Bach
(1735–1762)

Franz Joseph Haydn
(1732–1809)

Wolfgang Amadeus Mozart
(1756–1791)

Ludwig van Beethoven
(1770–1827)

ARTISTS

Louis de Carmontelle
(1717–1806)

Thomas Gainsborough
(1727–1788)

Francisco Göya
(1746–1828)

Jacques-Louis David
(1748–1825)

Elisabeth Vigée-Lebrun
(1755–1842)

AUTHORS

Voltaire
(1694–1778)

Benjamin Franklin
(1706–1790)

William Wordsworth
(1770–1850)

Jane Austen
(1775–1817)

VOCABULARY

Classical period

chamber music

symphony

crescendo

decrescendo

sonata-allegro form

Music of the Classical Period

The music of the Classical period was based on balance, clarity and simplicity. Like the architecture of ancient Greece, music was fit together in "building blocks" by balancing one four-bar phrase against another. Classical music was more restrained than the music of the Baroque period, when flamboyant embellishments were common.

The piano replaced the harpsichord and became a favorite instrument of composers. Many concertos were written for the piano. The string quartet was a popular form of **chamber music** *(music performed by a small instrumental ensemble, generally with one instrument per part)*. The **symphony** *(a large-scale work for orchestra)* was also a common type of music during this period. Orchestras continued to develop and expand into four families: brass, percussion, strings and woodwinds. Other forms, such as the opera, mass and oratorio, continued to develop as well.

Two major composers associated with the Classical period are Franz Joseph Haydn (1732–1809) and Wolfgang Amadeus Mozart (1756–1791). A third major composer, Ludwig van Beethoven (1770–1827), began composing during this period. Beethoven's works bridge the gap between the Classical and Romantic periods, and are discussed in the next period.

Performance Links

When performing music of the Classical period, it is important to apply the following guidelines:

- Listen for the melody line so the accompaniment parts do not overshadow it.
- Sing chords in tune.
- Make dynamic level changes that move smoothly through each **crescendo** *(a dynamic marking that indicates to gradually sing or play louder)* and **decrescendo** *(a dynamic marking that indicates to gradually sing or play softer)*.
- Keep phrases flowing and connected.

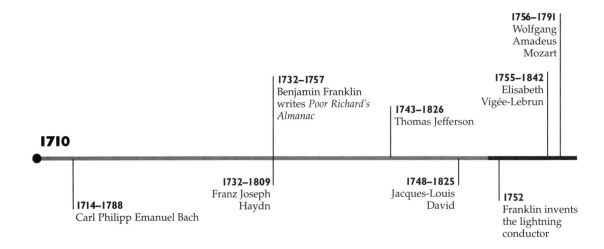

Listening Links

CHORAL SELECTION

"The Heavens Are Telling" from Creation by Franz Joseph Haydn (1732–1809)

Franz Joseph Haydn was an Austrian composer who was Beethoven's teacher, and Mozart's friend. The *Creation* is an oratorio based on a poem from John Milton's *Paradise Lost* and the first chapters of the book of Genesis from the Bible. The angels Gabriel, Uriel and Raphael are portrayed by three soloists, and they describe events of each day of the creation. "The Heavens Are Telling" is a grand celebration of praise that alternates between the full chorus and the trio of soloists. List the order of the choral voice parts in the imitative section as they enter with the words, "With wonders of His work."

INSTRUMENTAL SELECTION

Eine Kleine Nachtmusik, First Movement by Wolfgang Amadeus Mozart (1756–1791)

Wolfgang Amadeus Mozart, another Austrian composer, began his musical career at an extremely early age. By the time he was four years old, Mozart had already mastered the keyboard, and by age five, he had written his first composition. Considered one of the greatest composers of all time, he composed 600 musical works.

The first movement of *Eine Kleine Nachtmusik* is written in **sonata-allegro form**, *a large ABA form consisting of three sections: exposition, development and recapitulation.* The Exposition (section A) presents two themes: (a) and (b). Next comes the Development section (section B). The Recapitulation is a return to the original theme (a). Listen to this selection and write down the name for each section of the sonata-allegro form as you hear it.

Check Your Understanding

1. List three major nonmusical changes that took place during the Classical period.

2. Describe the characteristics of Classical music heard in *Eine Kleine Nachtmusik*.

3. Describe how music from the Classical period is different from music of the Baroque period.

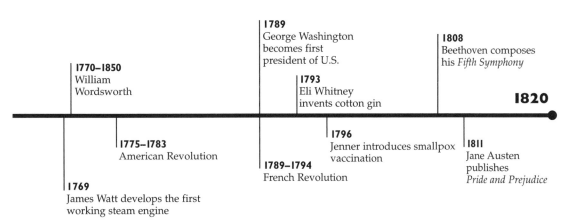

1789
George Washington becomes first president of U.S.

1808
Beethoven composes his *Fifth Symphony*

1770–1850
William Wordsworth

1793
Eli Whitney invents cotton gin

1820

1775–1783
American Revolution

1796
Jenner introduces smallpox vaccination

1811
Jane Austen publishes *Pride and Prejudice*

1789–1794
French Revolution

1769
James Watt develops the first working steam engine

MUSIC&ART | The American artist George Caleb Bingham (1811–1879) was born in Virginia and raised in Missouri. He became known for his river scenes, often of boatmen bringing cargo to the American West along the Missouri and Mississippi rivers. The scene here is a group of boatmen on a flatboat amusing themselves with their own music and dancing.

George Caleb Bingham. *The Jolly Flatboatmen.* 1846. Oil on canvas. 96.9 x 123.2 cm (38 1/8 x 48 1/2"). National Gallery of Art, Washington, D. C. Private Collection.

Focus

- Describe the Romantic period, including important developments.
- Describe characteristics of Romantic music.

The Romantic Period— A Time of Drama

A new sense of political and artistic freedom emerged during the **Romantic period** *(1820–1900)*. The period began in the middle of the Industrial Revolution, a time when manufacturing became mechanized and many people left farm life to work and live in cities where the manufacturing plants were located. Scientific and mechanical achievements were made in the development of railroads, steamboats, the telegraph and telephone, photography, and sound recordings.

The Industrial Revolution caused a major change in the economic and social life of the common people and also produced a wealthy middle class. More people were able to take part in cultural activities, such as attending music performances and going to art museums. Musicians and artists experienced greater freedom to express their individual creative ideas. This was because they were able to support themselves by ticket sales or sales of their art, instead of relying on the patronage of royalty or the church.

As people moved into the cities, nature and life in the country became the inspiration for many artists. The paintings of William Turner expressed the feelings suggested by nature. Later, French Impressionistic painters, including Claude Monet and Pierre-Auguste Renoir, developed new techniques bringing nature and natural light alive for the viewer.

Some of the most prominent thinkers and creators of this period were:

- Georges Bizet—French composer
- George Caleb Bingham—American painter
- Charles Dickens—English author
- Samuel F. B. Morse—American inventor who developed the telegraph

COMPOSERS

Ludwig van Beethoven (1770–1827)

Franz Schubert (1797–1828)

Felix Mendelssohn (1809–1847)

Frédéric Chopin (1810–1849)

Franz Liszt (1811–1886)

Richard Wagner (1813–1883)

Giuseppe Verdi (1813–1901)

Bedrich Smetana (1824–1884)

Johannes Brahms (1833–1897)

Georges Bizet (1838–1875)

Peter Ilyich Tchaikovsky (1840–1893)

Antonín Dvořák (1841–1904)

Claude Debussy (1862–1918)

ARTISTS

George Caleb Bingham (1811–1879)

Edgar Degas (1834–1917)

Paul Cezanne (1839–1906)

Auguste Rodin (1840–1917)

Claude Monet (1840–1926)

Pierre-Auguste Renoir (1841–1919)

Mary Cassatt (1845–1926)

Paul Gauguin (1848–1903)

Vincent van Gogh (1853–1890)

AUTHORS

Alexandre Dumas (1802–1870)

Henry Wadsworth Longfellow (1807–1882)

Charles Dickens (1812–1870)

Jules Verne (1828–1905)

Louisa May Alcott (1832–1884)

Mark Twain (1835–1910)

Rudyard Kipling (1865–1905)

VOCABULARY

Romantic period

music critic

overture

symphonic poem

Music of the Romantic Period

Music of the Romantic period focused on both the heights and depths of human emotion. The new musical ideas were expressed through larger works with complex vocal melodies and colorful harmonies. During this time, most of the brass and woodwind instruments developed into what they are today, and these instruments were used to add more tone and depth to the music.

Composers began to think about selling their music to the new audiences of middle-class people. Two types of music that appealed to these audiences were the extravagant spectacles of opera and the boldness of grand symphonic music. As music became public, it became subject to public scrutiny, particularly by music critics. A **music critic** is *a writer who gives an evaluation of a musical performance.*

Much of the music of the time was related to literature, such as Felix Mendelssohn's (1809–1847) *A Midsummer Night's Dream*, which was based on the play by William Shakespeare. A well-known section of this work is the **overture**, or *a piece for orchestra that serves as an introduction to an opera or other dramatic work.* The **symphonic poem** is *a single-movement work for orchestra, inspired by a painting, play or other literary or visual work.* Franz Liszt (1811–1886) was a prominent composer of this style of music. The Romantic period was also a time of nationalism, which was reflected in works such as Liszt's *Hungarian Dances*, Richard Wagner's focus on Germanic music, and the tributes to Italy found in Giuseppe Verdi's operas.

Performance Links

When performing music of the Romantic period, it is important to apply the following guidelines:

- Understand the relation of the text to the melody and harmony.
- Concentrate on phrasing, and maintain a clear, beautiful melodic line.
- Perform accurately the wide range of dynamics and tempos.
- Sing confidently in foreign languages to reflect nationalism in music.

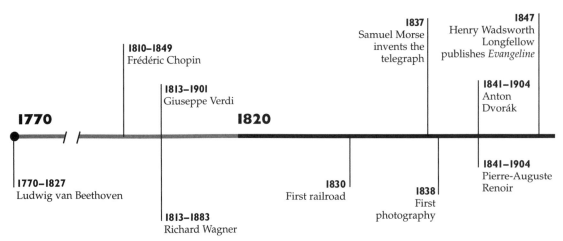

Listening Links

CHORAL SELECTION
"Toreador Chorus" from Carmen by Georges Bizet (1838–1875)

Carmen, by French composer Georges Bizet, is considered to be one of the most popular operas ever written. The opera tells the story of a gypsy girl who is arrested when she gets into a fight. Placed in the custody of the soldier Don Jose, Carmen soon entices him into a love affair. She then meets Escamilio, a toreador (bullfighter), and tries to get rid of Don Jose. Jilted, Don Jose stabs Carmen and kills himself. The "Toreador Chorus" is heard during the Procession of the Bullfighters. As you listen to the music, write two or three sentences to describe this procession scene in the opera as you think it would look.

INSTRUMENTAL SELECTION
"The Moldau" by Bedrich Smetana (1824–1884)

Bedrich Smetana was a prominent Czech composer. Smetana had a passion for music and composed in spite of his father's desire for him to become a lawyer. His musical efforts were focused mainly on trying to produce Czech national music based on the folk songs and dances that already existed. Smetana awoke one morning to find himself totally deaf. This created a depression that stayed with him through the remainder of his life. "The Moldau" represents Smetana's deep feeling about the beauty and significance of the river that flows through the city of Prague.

Check Your Understanding

1. List three major nonmusical changes that took place during the Romantic period.

2. Describe how "The Moldau" reflects nationalism in music of the Romantic period.

3. Describe how music of the Romantic period is different from music of another period.

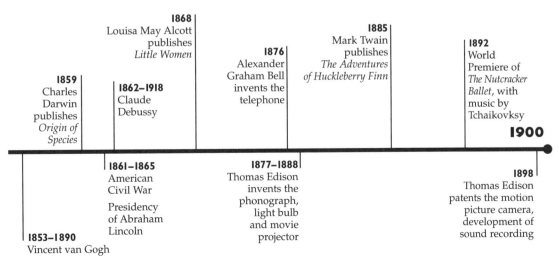

1859 Charles Darwin publishes *Origin of Species*

1853–1890 Vincent van Gogh

1868 Louisa May Alcott publishes *Little Women*

1862–1918 Claude Debussy

1861–1865 American Civil War / Presidency of Abraham Lincoln

1876 Alexander Graham Bell invents the telephone

1877–1888 Thomas Edison invents the phonograph, light bulb and movie projector

1885 Mark Twain publishes *The Adventures of Huckleberry Finn*

1892 World Premiere of *The Nutcracker Ballet*, with music by Tchaikovksy

1900

1898 Thomas Edison patents the motion picture camera, development of sound recording

**MUSIC & ART**

African American artist Romare Howard Bearden (1911–1988) is recognized as one of the most creative visual artists of the twentieth century. He experimented with many different styles and mediums but found a unique form of expression in collage. He had a great interest in literature, history, music, mathematics and the performing arts.

Romare Bearden. *The Piano Lesson (Homage to Mary Lou)*. 1983. Color lithograph on paper. 75.2 x 52.3 cm (29 1/2 x 20 1/2"). The Pennsylvania Academy of the Fine Arts, Philadelphia, Pennsylvania. The Harold A. and Ann R. Sorgenti Collection of Contemporary African American Art.

Focus

- Describe the Contemporary period, including important developments.
- Describe characteristics of Contemporary music.

The Contemporary Period— The Search for Originality

Nothing characterizes the **Contemporary period** *(1900–present)* better than technology. Many technological advances began on October 4, 1957, when the Soviet Union successfully launched *Sputnik I*, the world's first artificial satellite. While the Sputnik launch was a single event, it marked the start of the Space Age and began many new political, military, technological and scientific developments.

Isolation was greatly reduced worldwide by developments in travel (rail, sea and air) and communication (telephone, radio, television and the Internet). It was also reduced as countries came together during World War I and World War II. Elements of cultures merged as people moved from their countries to various parts of the world for economic, political or social reasons. It no longer seems strange, for example, to see Chinese or Mexican restaurants in most communities in the United States or McDonald's® restaurants in Europe and Asia.

Some of the noteworthy leaders of this period have been:

- Igor Stravinsky—Russian/American composer
- Romare Bearden—American artist
- Robert Frost—American poet
- Wilbur and Orville Wright—American inventors who designed and flew the first airplane
- Albert Einstein—German/American scientist who formulated theories of relativity

COMPOSERS

Sergei Rachmaninoff (1873–1943)

Arnold Schoenberg (1874–1951)

Béla Bartók (1881–1945)

Igor Stravinsky (1882–1971)

Sergey Prokofiev (1891–1953)

Carl Orff (1895–1982)

Aaron Copland (1900–1990)

Benjamin Britten (1913–1976)

Leonard Bernstein (1918–1990)

Moses Hogan (1957–2003)

ARTISTS

Henri Matisse (1869–1954)

Pablo Picasso (1881–1973)

Wassily Kandinsky (1866–1944)

Marc Chagall (1887–1985)

Georgia O'Keeffe (1887–1986)

Romare Howard Bearden (1911–1988)

Andy Warhol (1930–1987)

AUTHORS

Robert Frost (1874–1963)

Virginia Woolf (1882–1941)

Ernest Hemingway (1899–1961)

Rachel Carson (1907–1964)

James Baldwin (1924–1997)

JK Rowling (b. 1965)

VOCABULARY

Contemporary period

synthesizer

twelve-tone music

aleatory music

fusion

Music of the Contemporary Period

Technology has had a large influence on Contemporary music. Most people have access to music via radio, television and recordings. Technology has also influenced the music itself. The invention of electrified and electronic instruments led many composers to experiment with the new sounds. One of the most important new instruments was the **synthesizer**, *a musical instrument that produces sounds electronically, rather than by the physical vibrations of an acoustic instrument.*

The Contemporary period has witnessed a number of musical styles. Maurice Ravel (1875–1937) and Claude Debussy (1862–1918), for example, wrote music in the Impressionist style, often describing an impression of nature. Some of the music of Igor Stravinsky (1882–1971) and others was written in a neo-Classical (or "new" classical) style. Other music was considered avant-garde (or unorthodox or experimental); this included Arnold Schoenberg's (1874–1951) **twelve-tone music**, *a type of music that uses all twelve tones of the scale equally.* Composers experimented with **aleatory music**, or *a type of music in which certain aspects are performed randomly and left to chance.*

In addition, composers began using the rhythms, melodies and texts of other cultures in their compositions in a trend called **fusion**, or *the act of combining various types and cultural influences of music into a new style.*

Performance Links

When performing music of the Contemporary period, it is important to apply the following guidelines:

- Sing on pitch, even in extreme parts of your range.
- Tune intervals carefully in the skips found in many melodic lines.
- Sing changing meters and unusual rhythm patterns precisely.
- Perform accurately the wide range of dynamics and tempos.

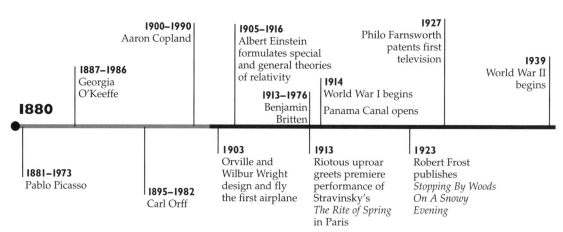

Listening Links

CHORAL SELECTION

"The Battle of Jericho," Traditional Spiritual, arranged by Moses George Hogan (1957–2003)

Moses Hogan, born in New Orleans, Louisiana, was a pianist, conductor and arranger. He has been one of the most influential arrangers of our time in the revitalization of the songs of our forebearers. His contemporary settings of African American spirituals have been revered by audiences and praised by critics. He had a unique talent for expanding the harmonies and rhythms while preserving the traditional essence of these spirituals. Hogan's arrangements have become staples in the repertoires of choirs worldwide. What specific musical effects did Hogan add in his arrangement of "The Battle of Jericho"?

INSTRUMENTAL SELECTION

"Infernal Dance of King Kaschei" from *The Firebird* by Igor Stravinsky (1882–1971)

Igor Stravinsky was born in Russia, but lived the last twenty-five years of his life in California. *The Firebird* is a ballet that begins when Prince Ivan gives a magical golden bird with wings of fire its freedom in return for a feather. With the help of the magic feather, Ivan conquers an evil king and frees the princesses and prisoners that the king had held captive. Prince Ivan falls in love with a princess and they live happily ever after.

In the first section of this piece, you can hear the loud shrieks of the firebird. How many times did you hear this sudden loud sound?

Check Your Understanding

1. List three major nonmusical changes that took place during the Contemporary period.

2. Discuss the differences between a composer and an arranger.

3. Describe how music of the Contemporary period is different from music of the Romantic period.

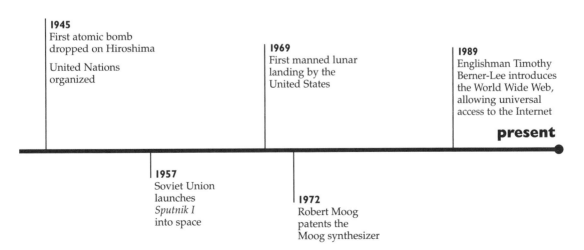

1945
First atomic bomb
dropped on Hiroshima

United Nations
organized

1957
Soviet Union
launches
Sputnik I
into space

1969
First manned lunar
landing by the
United States

1972
Robert Moog
patents the
Moog synthesizer

1989
Englishman Timothy
Berner-Lee introduces
the World Wide Web,
allowing universal
access to the Internet

present

SPOTLIGHT

Musical Theater

There are many ways to tell a story. You may share a story with others through storytelling, acting, drawing and even singing. When you add music and drama to the telling of a story, the storytelling becomes musical theater. **Musical theater** is *an art form that combines acting, singing and dancing to tell a story.* It also often includes staging, costumes, lighting and scenery.

The Broadway musical is an American invention. In reaction to the dramatic and often "stuffy" operas of the time, Americans invented their own version of musical theater that was less grandiose and spoke directly to the people. As New York City became a center of the arts and music, many musical theaters appeared on a street named Broadway. As a result, the word *Broadway* came to be identified with stage and music productions.

Broadway musicals blossomed during the 1920s and 1930s with the works of George Gershwin, Cole Porter and Irving Berlin. By the 1950s, the Broadway musical was well established. The composer/lyricist team of Frederick Lowe and Alan Jay Lerner wrote *My Fair Lady* (1956) and *Camelot* (1961). Some of the masterpieces created by the team of Richard Rodgers and Oscar Hammerstein II include *Oklahoma!* (1943), *Carousel* (1945) and *The Sound of Music* (1959). More recently, the composers Andrew Lloyd Webber and Stephen Sondheim have contributed to the continued success of Broadway musicals. Lloyd Webber's *Cats* (1981) and *The Phantom of the Opera* (1988) are two of the longest-running musicals in Broadway history.

Many are involved in the production of a Broadway musical, but it is the performers who bring the story to life through their singing, dancing and acting. If you have seen a musical or performed in one, you know how exciting it can be. For many, musical theater is indeed storytelling at its best!

Choral Library

Castle On A Cloud

Composer: Claude-Michel Schönberg, arranged by Linda Spevacek
Text: Alain Boublil, Jean-Marc Natel, and Herbert Kretzmer
Voicing: 2-Part

VOCABULARY

musical

head voice

legato

minor scale

Focus

- Extend the vocal range.

- Read and write melodic patterns based on the natural minor scale.

- Perform music from the musical theater.

Getting Started

Imagine living in a dark and dirty place. You own only one set of clothes, and they are filthy. It has been a long time since you've been allowed to bathe, wash your hair or brush your teeth. You are forced to work all day, clearing and wiping tables, sweeping and mopping floors, and washing and drying dishes. No one ever says, "Thank you." Instead, the people you live with shout commands at you and hurl insults at you. How long would it take before you would begin to dream of a better place to live?

 **SPOTLIGHT**

To learn more about musical theater, see page 126.

◆ History and Culture

"Castle On A Cloud" is a well-known song from the popular musical *Les Misérables*. A **musical** is *a play or film in which the story is expressed through speaking, acting, singing and dancing*. Based on the novel written by French author Victor Hugo (1802–1885), the musical *Les Misérables* premiered in Paris in 1980 and made its American debut in New York in 1987. In the musical, "Castle On A Cloud" is sung by an orphan named Cosette. She is sent to live with the Thenardiers, a couple who force her to be their servant. Cosette's life is very dreary and sad. The words of "Castle On A Cloud" express Cosette's wish for a better life.

Links to Learning

◆ **Vocal**

Perform the following example to practice singing in your **head voice**, or *the higher part of your singing range*. Sing in a **legato**, or *a connected and sustained style of singing*.

la   la   la   la   la   la   la   la_____
There is   a   cas - tle   on   a   cloud,_____

la   la   la   la   la   la   la   la_____
I   like to   go   there in   my   sleep._____

Now, read and perform the example below. Keep the same head-voice quality while singing these lower pitches.

la   la   la   la   la   la   la   la_____
Not in   my   cas - tle   on   a   cloud._____

◆ **Theory**

This arrangement is in the key of C minor and is based on the C minor scale. A **minor scale** is *a scale that has la as its keynote or home tone*. To locate "C" on a piano, find any set of two black keys. "C" is the white key just to the left. This scale uses the notes C, D, E♭, F, G A♭, B♭, C. Using the keyboard below as a guide, play the C minor scale.

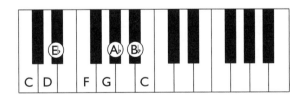

Evaluation

Demonstrate how well you have learned the skills and concepts featured in the lesson "Castle On A Cloud" by completing the following:

• With the help of a piano, find the highest note in your own vocal range that can be sung relaxed, sustained and with accurate pitch.

• Write a four-measure melody that is based on the C minor scale. Begin and end your piece on *la*, or C. Trade compositions with a classmate, and sight-sing each other's melodies. How accurate was your work?

(From "LES MISÉRABLES")
Castle On A Cloud
For 2-Part and Piano with Optional Glockenspiel or Bells

Arranged by
LINDA STEEN SPEVACEK

Music by CLAUDE-MICHEL SCHÖNBERG
Lyrics by HERBERT KRETZMER
Original Text by ALAIN BOUBLIL
and JEAN-MARC NATEL

Aren't an-y floors for me to sweep,_____ not in my cas - tle

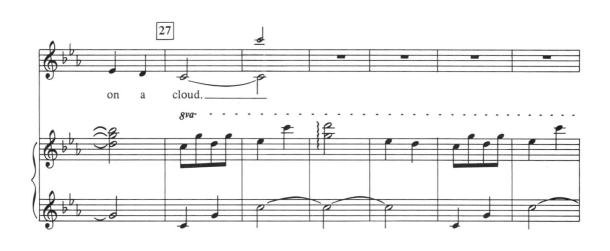

on a cloud._____

Part I

There is a room that's full of toys._____

Part II

There is a room that's full of toys._____

Dance of the One-Legged Sailor

Composer: Brent Pierce
Text: Brent Pierce
Voicing: SA

VOCABULARY

mixed meter

sea chantey

$\frac{5}{8}$ meter

Focus

- Read and perform music in mixed meter.
- Read and perform music in $\frac{5}{8}$ meter.
- Relate music to other subjects.

Getting Started

Have you ever injured your leg or ankle and had to walk with crutches or in a cast? Did you have to walk differently? Was your walk even or uneven? Were you able to dance or run? Composer Brent Pierce has written "Dance of the One-Legged Sailor" in **mixed meter**, *a technique in which the time signature changes frequently within a piece.* Mixed meter is used in this song to musically portray the uneven steps of the sailor.

◆ History and Culture

"Dance of the One-Legged Sailor" is written in the style of a sea chantey. A **sea chantey** is *a song sung by sailors, usually in the rhythm of their work.* The origin of chanteys is difficult to trace, due to the fact that much of this music has been taught by oral tradition. Chanteys were popular during the nineteenth century. These songs, which often told stories, may have been accompanied by instruments, such as harmonicas, violins or accordions. Since life at sea was hard in those days, singing helped to raise the sailors' spirits. It would not have been uncommon for them to sing while doing tasks such as turning sails or raising anchors. As you learn and perform "Dance of the One-Legged Sailor," think of tasks you might do on a ship while singing a chantey.

SKILL BUILDERS

To learn more about mixed meter, see Intermediate Sight-Singing, *page 97.*

Links to Learning

◆ Theory

$\frac{5}{8}$ **meter** is *a time signature in which there are five beats per measure and the eighth note receives the beat*. In this song, the use of $\frac{5}{8}$ meter is organized into two groupings: one set of three eighth notes and one set of two eighth notes per measure. Read and perform the example below.

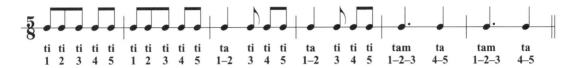

In mixed meter, the time signatures change frequently throughout a song. Read and perform the example below to practice rhythmic patterns in mixed meter. The eighth note should remain constant, and the beat should be steady throughout.

◆ Artistic Expression

The storyteller sings, "He's a man who loved to laugh and sing till one day he lost his leg." How did this happen? Imagine you are that sailor. Write a letter to your family back home about your adventures on the open seas.

Evaluation

Demonstrate how well you have learned the skills and concepts featured in the lesson "Dance of the One-Legged Sailor" by completing the following:

- With a small group, sing measures 9–18 to show that you can perform music in mixed meter. Were you able to sing the rhythms correctly? Were there any problem areas?

- Be an actor! In the character of the sailor, read your letter to the class. Evaluate your performance based on stage presence, clear diction and the ability to stay in the character of the sailor.

To my son Michael

Dance of the One-Legged Sailor

For SA and Piano

Words and Music by
BRENT PIERCE

138   Intermediate Treble

mates.

mates.

Now ye   mates   come heed my   warn - ing.   Don't

Now ye   mates   come heed my   warn - ing.   Don't

Lis-ten ye now to the whis-per of the north wind. Dance.

Heave way. Don't be late. Dance.

1. f
2. p

1. f
2. p

Come ye now, mates, and set sail to the wind.

Come ye now, mates, and set sail to the wind.

f

8va - - -

Dodi Li

Composer: Nira Chen, arranged by Doreen Rao
Text: Song of Solomon
Voicing: 2-Part

VOCABULARY

rondo form

minor scale

common time

 SKILL BUILDERS

To learn more about the key of E minor, see Intermediate Sight-Singing, *pages 91–94.*

Focus

- Describe and perform rondo form.

- Read and notate music based on the minor scale.

- Perform music that represents the Israeli culture.

Getting Started

Israeli violinist and conductor Pinchas Zuckerman often tells about his experience of conducting an orchestra made up of young people from around the world. He shares that although the musicians spoke different languages, they were able to communicate through the music and present a beautiful concert.

For a reason such as this, music is sometimes called the "universal language." When you sing or hear a song in a foreign language, you can still understand the spirit of the piece. For example, the energy and beauty of "Dodi Li" can be felt through the music and the flow of the Hebrew language.

◆ History and Culture

"Dodi Li" is an Israeli love song based on a text from the Old Testament book Song of Solomon. This arrangement is written in rondo form. In **rondo form**, *a repeated section is separated by several contrasting sections.* If you were to divide this song into sections, it would look like this: A, B, A, C, A, D, A. Find the repeated "A" sections in the music.

Doreen Rao, the arranger of this piece, went to Israel to work with a group of young singers. She had this to say: "During that special visit, I fell in love with the spirit and the musicality of Israeli choristers and their devotion to choral singing." Hopefully, you will share a similar experience of joy and musicality as you learn "Dodi Li."

Links to Learning

◆ Vocal

This arrangement is in the key of E minor and is based on the E minor scale. A **minor scale** is *a scale that has* la *as its keynote or home tone*. To locate "E" on the piano, find any set of two black keys. "E" is the white key just to the right. This scale uses the notes E, F♯, G A, B, C, D, E. Using the keyboard below as a guide, play the E minor scale.

Sing the E minor scale.

Copy the following examples onto a piece of staff paper. Write the correct solfège name under each pitch. Sing each example you have written. Then, locate the examples in your music.

◆ Theory

Of all the time signatures, $\frac{4}{4}$ meter is the most common. For this reason, **common time** is *another name for* $\frac{4}{4}$ *meter*. Both meters indicate four beats per measure with the quarter note receiving the beat. Common time is indicated by the symbol **C**. Look through your book and find other songs that are written in common time.

Evaluation

Demonstrate how well you have learned the skills and concepts featured in the lesson "Dodi Li" by completing the following:

- Demonstrate an understanding of rondo form by creating a movement for each section. The movement for section A should always be the same. How can this activity help you learn rondo form?

- Perform measures 3–6 of "Dodi Li" using solfège syllables to show that you can read a passage based on the minor scale. How did you do?

Dedicated to the Jeruslaem Music Center

Dodi Li

Israeli Song

For 2-Part and Piano

Arranged by
DOREEN RAO

Words from the SONG OF SONGS 2:16, 3:1, 4:9, 4:16
Music by NIRA CHEN

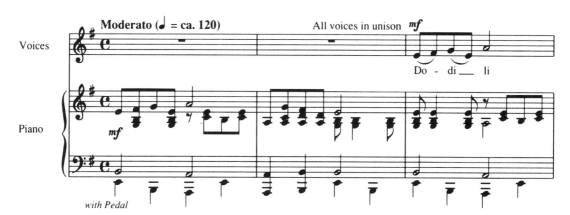

All voices in unison

43

Do - di li va - a - ni lo Ha - ro - e Ba-sho-sha-nim.

Treble I

47

Do - di li va - ni lo Ha - ro - e _____ Ba - sho-sha-nim.

Treble II

Do - di li va-ni lo Ha - ro - e Ba-sho-sha-nim.

Treble I

51

Do - di li va - ni lo Ha - ro - e _____ Ba - sho-sha-nim.

Treble II

Do - di li va - a - ni lo _____ Ha - ro - e Ba-sho-sha-nim.

rit.

sfz

150 **Intermediate Treble**

For A Child

Composer: James Mulholland
Text: Fannie Stearns Davis
Voicing: SA (Opt. SSA)

VOCABULARY

legato

rallentando

a tempo

Focus

- Observe tempo markings while performing.
- Use drama to reflect the meaning of the text.

Getting Started

And you shall run and wander,

And you shall dream and sing

Of brave things and bright things

Beyond the swallow's wings.

Words fit together in well-constructed poetry just like individual pieces of a patchwork quilt. Poetry might be thought of as a quilt of words. A verse is not complete without the unique shape and rhythm of each syllable. As a quilt is being crafted, the color and design choices of the maker add a personalized style.

Read the poem above. Picture an adult saying these words to a child. Where is this event taking place? Who is the adult and who is the child? As you learn this beautiful song, keep in mind who you are and to whom you are speaking. Using these thoughts will help you choose the style, emphasis and color to make the patchwork of words fit together seamlessly.

 **SPOTLIGHT**

To learn more about concert etiquette, see page 71.

◆ History and Culture

"For A Child" is based on the sixteenth-century Irish folk tune "Slane" (named after a famous hill in Ireland). It serves as the melody of the well-known hymn "Be Thou My Vision." In contrast, the text of "For A Child" was written by American poet Fannie Stearns Davis in the early twentieth century. In addition to this text, she published two volumes of poetry between 1913 and 1915.

Links to Learning

◆ Vocal

Sing the E♭ major scale with a beautiful **legato** (*connected and sustained*) tone. Then, in a circle of three to four singers, choose one singer to sing *do*. Continuing to sing in a legato style, pass the scale along by having the next singer sing *re*, the next *mi*, and so on. Practice the scale ascending and descending in this manner, having a different singer start the scale each time.

E♭	F	G	A♭	B♭	C	D	E♭	D	C	B♭	A♭	G	F	E♭
do	re	mi	fa	sol	la	ti	do	ti	la	sol	fa	mi	re	do

Perform the following example to practice the melodic skips and wide vocal range used in "For A Child." Apply the tempo changes **rallentando** (*a marking that indicates to gradually get slower*) and **a tempo** (*a marking that indicates to return to original tempo*) as you sing.

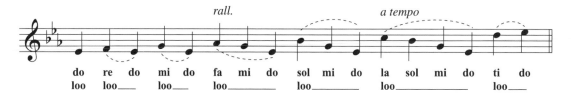

do	re	do	mi	do	fa	mi	do	sol	mi	do	la	sol	mi	do	ti	do
loo	loo___		loo___		loo___			loo___			loo___				loo___	

◆ Artistic Expression

Recite the text of "For A Child" as a poem. Make a list of historical characters that might have spoken these words to a child (e.g., a teacher, a governess, a pioneer mother). Try speaking the words as that character. Which words did you emphasize? Now give your character an age (e.g., 21, 50, 75) and place your character in a setting (e.g., at a family reunion, at a birthday party, on a covered wagon). Recite the words again. What did you change? Reflect on these ideas as you sing this song.

Evaluation

Demonstrate how well you have learned the skills and concepts featured in the lesson "For A Child" by completing the following:

- With a group of four to six classmates, sing measures 1–18, observing tempo markings. Take turns serving as the conductor. How did you do?

- Referring to the Artistic Expression section above, bring in one prop to identify your character. Use the prop as you sing measures 27–44 in character. Be an attentive audience as others perform and use proper concert etiquette.

Commissioned by the 1999 Southwestern ACDA Children's Honor Choir
Henry Leck, Director
With the generous support of a Butler University Grant

For A Child

For SA (Opt. SSA) and Piano

Words by
FANNIE STEARNS DAVIS

Music by
JAMES MULHOLLAND
(based on a 16th century Irish melody)

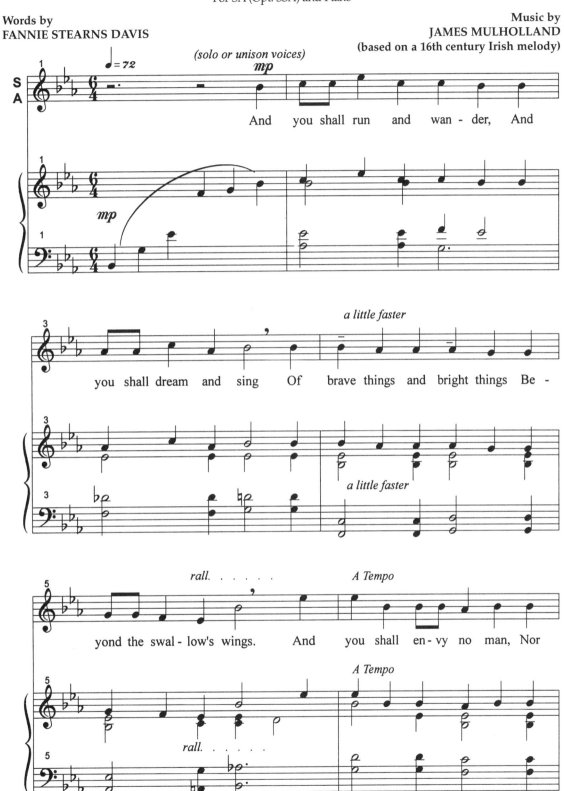

hurt your heart with sighs, For I will keep you sim - ple That

God may make you wise. Your friends shall be the tall wind, The

* even eighth notes
stems indicates hands

riv - er and the tree; The Sun that laughs and march - es, The

you shall en-vy no man, Nor hurt your heart with sighs, For

I will keep you sim - ple That God may make you

wise._____ And

you shall run and wan-der, And you shall dream and

sing.

The Fox

Composer: Traditional Folk Song, arranged by Kirk C. Aamot
Text: Traditional
Voicing: 2-Part

VOCABULARY

folk song

narrative song

diction

head voice

$\frac{2}{4}$ meter

 **SKILL BUILDERS**

To learn more about $\frac{2}{4}$ *meter, see* Intermediate Sight-Singing, *page 61.*

Focus

- Read complex rhythmic notation in $\frac{2}{4}$ meter.
- Relate music to storytelling.
- Perform expressively using the head voice and clear diction.

Getting Started

Stories are shared in many different ways. They may be written in books, told in the oral tradition from one person to another, or even viewed in a movie. Stories may also be told through singing. For centuries, people have put their stories to music. Think of songs you know that tell a story. Find examples of story-telling songs in this book.

◆ History and Culture

Folk songs are *songs that have been passed down from generation to generation through oral tradition and often describe a certain place or event.* There are many different types of folk songs. *A folk song that tells a story* is sometimes called a **narrative song**. The subject matter may be real or imagined. "The Fox" is a narrative song that tells a fictional story about a fox and his quest to find supper for his large family. He decides to raid the henhouse of a nearby farm. The story has a happy ending for the fox and his family, but not so happy for the goose and farmer John.

Although the exact origins of "The Fox" are unknown, it is believed to be a folk song from Europe that was brought to the United States by the early settlers. Enjoy learning this narrative song that has been a part of American folklore for over two hundred years.

Links to Learning

◆ Vocal

Read and perform the following example to help develop the crisp **diction** (*the pronunciation of words while singing*) needed to clearly express the text of "The Fox."

zing - a - zing - a - zee, zing - a - zing - a - zee, zing - a - zing - a - zing - a - zing - a - zee
pit - ter pat - ter pit, pit - ter pat - ter pat, pit - ter pat - ter pit - ter pat - ter pit

Perform the following melodic pattern to practice singing in your **head voice,** or *the higher part of your singing range.* Raise the pitch one half step on each repetition.

ee   oh

◆ Theory

Read and perform the following example to practice reading rhythmic patterns with sixteenth notes in $\frac{2}{4}$ meter. In $\frac{2}{4}$ **meter,** there are *two beats per measure and the quarter note receives the beat.*

ti   ti   ti   ti   ti ti ka ti ti ka   ti ka ti ka ti ka ti ka   ti   ti   tim   ka   ta   ta

◆ Artistic Expression

To develop artistry through storytelling, practice reading the lyrics of "The Fox" using inflection in your voice to reflect the various characters in the story. Be dramatic in your expressions. Tell your story to a friend or family member.

Evaluation

Demonstrate how well you have learned the skills and concepts featured in the lesson "The Fox" by completing the following:

• Chant the rhythm in measures 6–20, to show your ability to read complex rhythmic patterns in $\frac{2}{4}$ meter. How did you do?

• Referring to the Artistic Expression section above, record yourself telling the story of "The Fox" and then singing the song. Compare both recordings. In what ways did you change your style of singing after reciting the story?

Dedicated to the Double Four Ranch cousins

The Fox

For 2-Part and Piano with Optional Fiddle*

Arranged by
KIRK C. AAMOT

Traditional Folk Song

*Fiddle part found on page 171.

* Cued notes throughout may be played if not using Fiddle.

* Exclaimed in a high-pitched, hysterical voice.

The Fox

FIDDLE

Traditional Folksong
Arranged by KIRK C. AAMOT

Freedom Is Coming

Composer: South African Folk Song, arranged by Henry Leck
Text: Traditional
Voicing: 3-Part Treble

VOCABULARY

oral tradition

improvisation

descant

intonation

tied notes

Focus

- Create improvisation.
- Compose and perform rhythmic patterns with tied notes.
- Perform music representing South African culture.

Getting Started

Some musical traditions rely on printed music. Others share music through the **oral tradition**, in which *music is learned through rote or by ear and is interpreted by its performer(s)*. "Freedom Is Coming" is from the country of South Africa and is an example of a song that has been learned through this oral tradition. Even though there is no definitive version of this song written down, arranger Henry Leck has provided a notated version for young choirs.

One common practice in South African music is the use of **improvisation**, or *the art of singing or playing music, making it up as you go*. As you learn "Freedom Is Coming," you may want to improvise and create your own interpretation of this song. For example, begin with the melody only, and after several repetitions, gradually add additional parts. Try adding a **descant** (*a special part that is often sung higher than the other parts*) or creating new verses. Above all, have fun and experiment!

 **SPOTLIGHT**

To learn more about improvisation, see page 104.

◆ History and Culture

For many years, South Africa was a place of hardship. From the late 1940s to the early 1990s, a ruling minority enforced a system of strict racial segregation known as apartheid. Native South Africans were denied the right to vote. Schools and churches were separate, based on race. After apartheid was dismantled, equal rights and freedom were restored. "Freedom Is Coming" was made popular during those years of struggle and oppression as a song of hope for better things to come.

Links to Learning

◆ Vocal

Read and perform the following example to practice singing the three-part harmony that is found in this song. Pay close attention to your **intonation**, or *in-tune singing*.

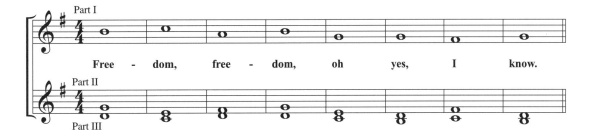

Free - dom, free - dom, oh yes, I know.

◆ Theory

Perform the following examples to practice reading rhythmic patterns with dotted and **tied notes**, or *two or more notes of the same pitch connected together to make one longer note*.

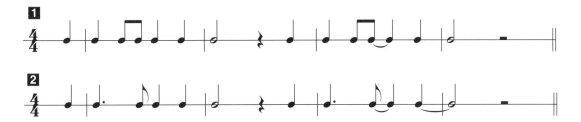

Evaluation

Demonstrate how well you have learned the skills and concepts featured in the lesson "Freedom Is Coming" by completing the following:

- Using the rhythmic patterns in the song as a guide, write a four-measure composition that includes dotted and tied notes. Perform your composition for the class. Were all the rhythms correct? Check your work.

- Improvise! While the rest of the choir sings "Freedom Is Coming," take turns improvising a short melodic passage during the sustained notes. Or, improvise a rhythmic pattern on a percussion instrument during the entire song. Evaluate how well you were able to improvise a melodic or rhythmic passage.

Freedom Is Coming

For 3-Part Treble, a cappella

Arranged by
HENRY LECK

Collected by
ANDERS NYBERG

174 Intermediate Treble

Great Day!

Composer: Traditional Spiritual, arranged by Rollo A. Dilworth
Text: Traditional
Voicing: 2-Part

VOCABULARY

spiritual

call and response

phrase

Focus

• Read and perform dotted rhythms accurately.

• Sing with appropriate phrasing and dynamic expression.

 **SKILL BUILDERS**

To learn more about dotted rhythms, see Intermediate Sight-Singing, *pages 45, 48 and 49.*

Getting Started

In your opinion, what is the difference between a good day and a great day? What images or ideas come to mind when you think about the characteristics of a great day? In this arrangement of the spiritual "Great Day!" you will have the opportunity to express the excitement of such a day.

◆ History and Culture

Spirituals are *songs that were first sung by African American slaves and are usually based on biblical themes or stories*. These songs were used as forms of expressing emotions such as sorrow, joy and hope. Spirituals were also a means of communication, often containing hidden messages. Like many traditional African American spirituals, "Great Day!" is a jubilant expression of joy and anticipation for the freedom and social justice to come.

This setting of "Great Day!" features **call and response,** which is when *a leader or group sings a phrase (call) followed by a response of the same or another phrase by another group*. This technique was often used in the creation and teaching of spirituals and is found in the verses of this arrangement. As the piece comes to its rousing conclusion, the opening melody returns in an improvisational style.

Links to Learning

◆ Vocal

A **phrase** is *a musical idea with a beginning and an end*. Read and perform the following example to practice singing a phrase similar to those in "Great Day!"

do   mi   sol   la   sol   fa   mi   re   do

◆ Theory

Read and perform the following example to practice rhythmic patterns found in "Great Day!," including dotted rhythms.

tam   ti ta   ti ka ti ka ta   ti ka ti ka ta   tam   ti ta   ti ka ti ka ta   ti ti ta

◆ Artistic Expression

Be the conductor! As the class sings the example below, take turns being the conductor. Through your conducting gestures, outline the shape of the phrase.

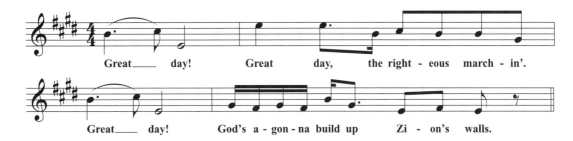

Great___ day!   Great   day,   the right - eous march - in'.

Great___ day!   God's a - gon - na build up   Zi - on's   walls.

Evaluation

Demonstrate how well you have learned the skills and concepts featured in the lesson "Great Day!" by completing the following:

- Clap measures 3–6 of "Great Day!" to show that you can read dotted rhythms accurately. Rate your performance on a scale of 1 to 5, with 5 being the best.

- Show that you can perform expressively by chanting the text and conducting the contour of a phrase. Were you able to do both at the same time? How can singing with shaped phrases improve your performance?

Commissioned by the Jubilate Children's Choir of the North Shore, Northfield, Illinois
Beverly Decker-Baar, Music Director

Great Day!

For 2-Part and Piano

Arranged by ROLLO A. DILWORTH

Traditional Spiritual

God spoke and the char - iot did stop.
we go march - in'___ through the land.

God's a - gon - na build up Zi - on's walls. This
I'll

, *sub.* *f*

is the day of ju - bi - lee.___
take my breast - plate, sword and shield.___
The
And

God's a - gon - na build up Zi - on's walls.

mf

Lord has set His peo - ple free.
march out bold - ly in the field.___

God's a - gon - na build up Zi - on's walls.

f

Kikkehihi

Composer: Johann Hermann Schein (1586–1630), edited by Thomas Juneau
Text: Johann Hermann Schein, English translation by Thomas Juneau
Voicing: 3-Part Treble

VOCABULARY

madrigal

polyphony

imitation

word painting

chest voice

 **SPOTLIGHT**

To learn more about the changing voice, see page 85.

Focus

- Define characteristics of and perform a madrigal.
- Read rhythmic patterns with dotted eighth and sixteenth notes.

Getting Started

Among the favorite songs of preschoolers is "Old MacDonald." Children love making the different animal sounds as they sing. "Kikkehihi" is a song about the morning cries of hens and roosters. It features much of the same charm as "Old MacDonald" but with a German flair. As you listen to and learn "Kikkehihi," you will discover how this music describes the sounds of an early morning on the farm.

◆ History and Culture

Johann Hermann Schein (1586–1630) lived in Germany during the Baroque period (1600–1750). Primarily a composer of vocal works, Schein wrote "Kikkehihi" in 1626. This song is an example of a **madrigal**, or *a secular part-song that was developed during the Renaissance period*. Generally secular in text, these songs are sometimes about animals or birds. Characteristic of the madrigal, "Kikkehihi" is written in a light and detached style.

Even though "Kikkehihi" is a short piece, Schein has used a variety of musical tools commonly found in madrigals to create its unique sound. First, this piece is an example of **polyphony**, in that there are *two or more different melodic lines being sung at the same time*. **Imitation**, or *the act of one part copying what another part has already sung*, is also found throughout the piece. Finally, **word painting**, or *a technique in which the music tries to depict the meaning of the words*, is used. Find examples of polyphony, imitation and word painting in the music.

Links to Learning

◆ **Vocal**

Perform the following examples to help develop your **chest voice**, or *the lower part of your singing range*, and to prepare you to sing "Kikkehihi."

Kik - ke - hi - hi,_____   Kik - ke - hi - hi._____
kee - kuh - hee - hee,_____   *kee - kuh - hee - hee._____*

◆ **Theory**

Read and perform the following dotted patterns used in "Kikkehihi." Form two groups. Have one group tap the steady beat while the other group claps the rhythmic patterns. Begin slowly. Gradually increase the speed as you are able. When you are secure in tapping or clapping your part, switch roles.

Evaluation

Demonstrate how well you have learned the skills and concepts featured in the lesson "Kikkehihi" by completing the following:

- In your own words, describe a *madrigal* and the various musical tools Schein has used in "Kikkehihi."

- In a trio with one student on a part, perform the rhythmic patterns in the song from measures 1–5. Based on rhythmic accuracy, rate your performance on a scale of 1 to 5, with 5 being the best.

Kikkehihi
from *Musica Boscareccia*

For 3-Part Treble, a cappella

Edited and Translated by
THOMAS JUNEAU

JOHANN HERMANN SCHEIN
(1586–1630)

Myoon-myoon

Composer: Stephen Leek (b. 1959)
Text: Stephen Leek
Voicing: SA

SPOTLIGHT

To learn more about posture, see page 29.

Focus

• Define and perform aleatory music.

• Relate music to other concepts.

• Perform music that represents the Aboriginal culture.

Getting Started

What places in the United States are important to us as a country? You may think of the Grand Canyon or the Smoky Mountains, with their natural beauty. Or, perhaps you may think of the Washington Monument or Independence Hall, with their historical significance. What other places can you think of?

If you are among the Aboriginal people of Australia, you would most likely think of a different list of places. "Myoon-myoon" is a song about those places.

◆ History and Culture

The Aboriginal people have lived in Australia's Northern Territory for thousands of years and are among the region's first inhabitants. Their culture is one of the oldest in the world. Almost all of the various geographical sites in the territory are sacred to the Aboriginal people. In "Myoon-myoon," composer Stephen Leek (b. 1959), attempts to musically portray the color and beauty of the Australian landscape. To better understand this piece, you will need to be familiar with the following words and place names:

• Myoon-myoon: Red earth

• Uluru: Traditional Aboriginal name for Ayer's Rock, the world's largest monolith (a formation made of a single stone)

• Olga sisters: Refers to the Olgas, a collection of smaller rock formations near Uluru

• Red heart: Another name for the center of Australia

Picture the beauty of Australia's Northern Territory as you sing "Myoon-myoon."

Links to Learning

◆ Vocal

"Myoon-myoon" was composed in the late twentieth century and is an example of **aleatory music**, or *chance music*. Like the name implies, certain aspects of this song are to be performed randomly.

To create this aleatoric sound, sing "ah-ee-oo" very smoothly and slowly on one pitch. Then, on the same pitch, sing "mah-ee" (as in the word "my") and connect it to "oon." Finally, experiment with different people singing these syllables randomly, or at their own tempo and starting at different times. The singing should sound chant-like.

Sometimes when the sound is focused just right, and the entire choir is on the same pitch, small whistle-like tones can be heard above the pitch everyone is singing. These are called **harmonics**, or *overtones*. Try and see if your choir can produce harmonics.

◆ Artistic Expression

To develop artistry through writing, research an aspect of the Aboriginal culture and write a paragraph about what you have learned. Some topics to choose from are music, art, language, food, famous people or geography.

Evaluation

Demonstrate how well you have learned the skills and concepts featured in lesson "Myoon-myoon" by completing the following:

- In your own words, define *aleatory music*. Then, with three or four classmates, create an aleatoric composition using the names of famous geographic sites in the United States. What characteristics of your composition can be found in "Myoon-myoon?"

- Share your paragraph on the Aboriginal culture with the class. As a class, decide which paragraph could be placed in the Program Notes for a performance. What did you learn?

Myoon-myoon
from *Ancient Cries*

For SA and Piano

Words and Music by
STEPHEN LEEK

Now's The Time

Composer: Charlie Parker (1920–1955), arranged by Norma Jean Luckey
Text: Scat Syllables
Voicing: SSA

scat singing

jazz

swing rhythms

syncopation

improvisation

 SPOTLIGHT

To learn more about vocal jazz, see page 91.

Focus

- Perform swing rhythms with precision and accuracy.
- Improvise by scat singing.
- Perform music representing the vocal jazz style.

Getting Started

Have you ever forgotten the words to a song while you were singing? Did you find yourself making up words or singing syllables that fit into the style of the music? If so, then you were scat singing. **Scat singing**, or *improvisational singing that uses nonsense syllables instead of words*, was made popular by jazz trumpeter Louis Armstrong (1901–1971). He would scat sing to imitate the sounds of the instruments in his band. In this arrangement of "Now's The Time," you will have the opportunity to scat sing.

◆ History and Culture

Developed in New Orleans in the early twentieth century, **jazz** is *an original American style of music that features swing rhythms, syncopation and improvisation.* **Swing rhythms** are *rhythms in which two even eighth notes are changed into uneven eighth notes.* The first note becomes longer than the second, and a triplet feel is created. **Syncopation** is *a rhythmic style that places the accent on a weak beat or the weak portion of a beat.* **Improvisation** is *the art of singing or playing music, making it up as you go.*

"Now's The Time" was written by Charlie Parker (1920–1955), a famous jazz alto saxophone player. His nickname was "Bird" because he loved to eat chicken. It was also a fitting name for him since his fingers flew over the keys of his instrument when he played.

Links to Learning

◆ Theory

Read and perform the following rhythmic patterns to understand and experience the relationship between triplets and swing eighth note patterns.

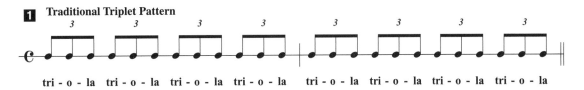

1 Traditional Triplet Pattern

tri - o - la tri - o - la tri - o - la tri - o - la   tri - o - la tri - o - la tri - o - la tri - o - la

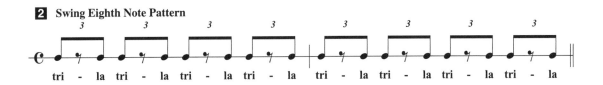

2 Swing Eighth Note Pattern

tri - la tri - la tri - la tri - la   tri - la tri - la tri - la tri - la

◆ Artistic Expression

In a small group, read and perform the following example, while keeping the beat steady and performing in a swing style. Notice the placement of accents on the weak beats and how this creates a syncopated feel.

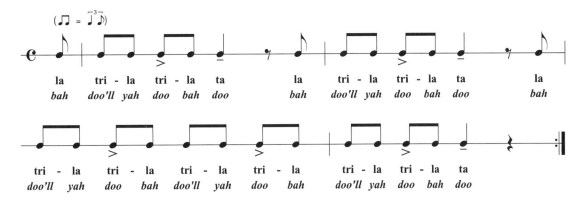

la   tri - la tri - la ta   la   tri - la tri - la ta   la
bah *doo'll yah* *doo* *bah* *doo* *bah* *doo'll yah* *doo* *bah* *doo* *bah*

tri - la tri - la tri - la tri - la   tri - la tri - la ta
doo'll *yah* *doo* *bah* *doo'll* *yah* *doo* *bah*   *doo'll yah* *doo* *bah* *doo*

Evaluation

Demonstrate how well you have learned the skills and concepts featured in the lesson "Now's The Time" by completing the following:

- Alone in a small group, chant the words in measures 2–10 in rhythm to show your ability to perform swing rhythms. Rate your performance on a scale of 1 to 5, with 5 being the best.

- In your own words, define *scat singing*. Then, create your own scat syllables for the melody in measures 15–23. Evaluate how you did.

To Doris Weaver and John Wilson

Now's The Time

For SSA and Piano

Arranged by
NORMA JEAN LUCKEY

Music by
CHARLIE PARKER (1920–1955)

* Equal division of voices on the two parts

The Star-Spangled Banner

Composer: John Stafford Smith (1750–1836), arranged by Emily Crocker
Text: Francis Scott Key (1780–1843)
Voicing: SSA

VOCABULARY

national anthem

accidental

 **SPOTLIGHT**

To learn more about careers in music, see page 77.

Focus

• Read music notation.

• Perform music that represents our American heritage.

Getting Started

Flags, mottos and anthems are all symbols of national pride and patriotism. Match the first line of each **national anthem** (*a patriotic song adopted by a nation through tradition or decree*) below to its corresponding country.

1. England   A. "… at the cry of battle lend your swords and bridle."

2. Mexico   B. "Ye sons of … awake to Glory! Hark! Hark! The people bid you rise!"

3. France   C. "God save our gracious queen. Long live our noble queen."

4. Japan   D. "Thousands of years of happy reign be thine."

And of course, "Oh say, can you see, by the dawn's early light…" are proud words for all Americans.

◆ History and Culture

During the War of 1812, a young American named Francis Scott Key (1780–1843) was on a ship during a British attack on Fort McHenry outside Baltimore, Maryland. An American flag with fifteen stars flew over the fort. The next morning, the flag, though battered and torn, was still there. Inspired by this sight, Key wrote the words to "The Star-Spangled Banner" on the back of a letter he had in his pocket. The melody of this song was written by English composer John Stafford Smith (1750–1836) in 1775, and was originally known as "To Anacreon in Heaven." Later, this tune was combined with Key's poem.

By the 1860s, "The Star-Spangled Banner" had the distinction of being performed at most patriotic occasions. However, Congress did not make it the national anthem of the United States until 1931.

Links to Learning

◆ Vocal

This arrangement is in the key of A♭ major and is based on the A♭ major scale. To locate "A♭" on a piano, find any set of three black keys. "A♭" is the middle black key. This scale uses the notes A♭, B♭, C, D♭, E♭, F, G, A♭. Using the keyboard below as a guide, play the A♭ major scale.

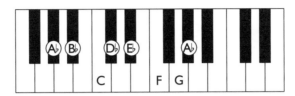

Sing the A♭ major scale.

| A♭ | B♭ | C | D♭ | E♭ | F | G | A♭ | G | F | E♭ | D♭ | C | B♭ | A♭ |
| do | re | mi | fa | sol | la | ti | do | ti | la | sol | fa | mi | re | do |

◆ Theory

Accidentals are *symbols used in music to change or alter pitches*. In "The Star-Spangled Banner," the pitch *fa* is sometimes raised to *fi*, and *sol* is sometimes raised to *si*. Analyze the music. Find the words or syllables that are sung on *fi* and *si*.

The solfège syllable *mi* is also common in a variety of melodic patterns. Sing each pattern below. Then, locate each pattern in the music. Identify the words or syllables for each pattern.

do to *mi*   *la* to *mi*   *sol* to *mi*   *mi* to *do*

◆ Artistic Expression

The text of "The Star-Spangled Banner" contains words that are no longer common. Write out the entire text and underline each word that is unfamiliar to you. With the help of a dictionary, define these words. Then, write the text out again. In place of each underlined word, insert your new definition.

Evaluation

Demonstrate how well you have learned the skills and concepts featured in the lesson "The Star-Spangled Banner" by completing the following:

- Sing your voice part of "The Star-Spangled Banner" using solfège syllables rather than words to show that you can read music notation. How did you do?

- Write an introduction to "The Star-Spangled Banner" to be read at a performance. Choose words appropriate to the patriotic style of this piece that will encourage your listeners to think of what America means to them.

The Star-Spangled Banner

For SSA, a cappella

Arranged by
EMILY CROCKER

Words by FRANCIS SCOTT KEY
Music by JOHN STAFFORD SMITH

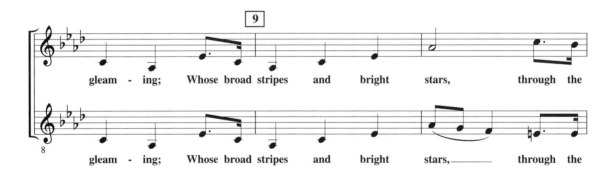

Winds Of Peace

Composer: Traditional Hebrew Round, arranged by Nancy Grundahl
Text: Traditional Hebrew, English Text by Nancy Grundahl
Voicing: 4-Part Treble

VOCABULARY

step-wise motion

skip-wise motion

head voice

Focus

• Write original lyrics.

• Perform a cappella music in small ensembles.

• Perform music representing the Israeli culture.

Getting Started

do do sol sol la la sol   fa fa mi mi re re do

This is a melody that lots of people know, but in different ways. In America, young children use this melody to sing "Twinkle, Twinkle Little Star" and "The ABC Song." But in France, children sing of their desire for candy to the same tune ("Ah! Vous dirai-je, Maman"). A melody can take on different meanings, based on the words used with it.

◆ History and Culture

When the melody is given new words, it surfaces with a fresh meaning or a different character. Such is the case with "Winds of Peace. "Composer Nancy Grundahl was captivated by the traditional Hebrew round "Ruach, Ruach" when she heard it performed by a young Israeli choir. Here is the translation of the Hebrew that inspired her English version of "Winds Of Peace."

Ruach, ruach, ruach, ruach,   *Spirit, spirit, spirit, spirit,*
lama lo tishkav la nuach   *Why don't you lay down to rest?*
min haboker tishtolel   *From the morning you are agitated*
vehine k'var bahaleil.   *And now the night is coming on.*

Perform this beautiful song with a supported and flowing vocal line. You may inspire someone in the audience to write another new set of words for "Winds Of Peace."

SKILL BUILDERS

To learn more about the key of A minor, see Intermediate Sight-Singing, *pages 20–22, 33–35, 68–72.*

Links to Learning

◆ Vocal

"Winds Of Peace" has a very flowing style because the melody contains **step-wise motion,** or *the movement from a given note to the next note above or below it on the staff.* However, there is also **skip-wise motion,** or *the movement from a given note to another note that is two or more notes above or below it on the staff.* Notice that some of these skips are very large. In the example below, find the six skips and sing each one using solfege syllables.

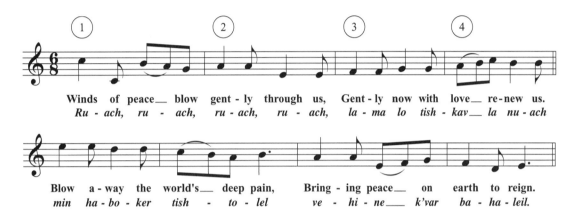

Winds of peace— blow gent - ly through us, Gent - ly now with love— re-new us.
Ru - ach, ru - ach, ru - ach, ru - ach, la - ma lo tish - kav— la nu - ach

Blow a - way the world's— deep pain, Bring - ing peace— on earth to reign.
min ha - bo - ker tish - to - lel ve - hi - ne— k'var ba - ha - leil.

Within a small group, perform "Winds Of Peace" in unison and then as a round. Sing all pitches in your **head voice** (*the higher part of the singer's vocal range*), using sustained breath support to help maintain the flowing style.

◆ Artistic Expression

The symbolic use of the word *wind* is a familiar poetic device. "Fly like the wind," "the winds of time," "the wind in your sails," and "may the wind be always at your back" all represent the gentle, constant force of the wind. Use your voice to express the quality of the wind.

Evaluation

Demonstrate how well you have learned the skills and concepts featured in the lesson "Winds Of Peace" by completing the following:

- Write a new verse for "Winds Of Peace" by using a symbolic representation for the wind. Perform your composition for the class. How important are the words to a song? In what ways did your new lyrics change your performance?

- In a small group, sing "Winds Of Peace" as a round. You may use the printed words, or your original new words. Record your performance and then evaluate how well your small group was able to sing a cappella.

Winds Of Peace
(Ruach, Ruach)

For 4-Part Treble and Piano with Optional Flute*

English Text by NANCY GRUNDAHL
Arranged by NANCY GRUNDAHL

Traditional Hebrew Round

*Flute part found on page 217.

Blow a-way the world's deep pain, Bring-ing peace on earth to reign.

Ped.   * Ped.   * sim.

21

Flute

mf espressivo

mf espressivo

tacet to m. 41   *ritard.*

* Divide voices so as to achieve four parts of equal timbre.

Winds Of Peace
(Ruach, Ruach)

FLUTE

Traditional Hebrew Round
Arranged by NANCY GRUNDAHL

Glossary

2/2 meter   A time signature in which there are two beats per measure and the half note receives the beat.

2/4 meter   A time signature in which there are two beats per measure and the quarter note receives the beat.

3/2 meter   A time signature in which there are three beats per measure and the half note receives the beat.

3/4 meter   A time signature in which there are three beats per measure and the quarter note receives the beat.

3/8 meter   A time signature in which there is one group of three eighth notes per measure and the dotted quarter note receives the beat. When the tempo is very slow, this meter can be counted as having three beats per measure, with the eighth note receiving the beat.

4/4 meter   A time signature in which there are four beats per measure and the quarter note receives the beat.

5/8 meter   A time signature in which there are five beats per measure and the eighth note receives the beat.

6/4 meter   A time signature in which there are two groups of three quarter notes per measure and the dotted half note receives the beat. When the tempo is very slow, this meter can be counted as having six beats per measure, with the quarter note receiving the beat.

6/8 meter   A time signature in which there are two groups of three eighth notes per measure and the dotted quarter note receives the beat. When the tempo is very slow, this meter can be counted as having six beats per measure, with the eighth note receiving the beat.

9/8 meter   A time signature in which there are three groups of three eighth notes per measure and the dotted quarter note receives the beat. When the tempo is very slow, this meter can be counted as having nine beats per measure, with the eighth note receiving the beat.

12/8 meter   A time signature in which there are four groups of three eighth notes per measure and the dotted quarter note receives the beat.

A

a cappella *(ah-kah-PEH-lah)*   [It.] A style of singing without instrumental accompaniment.

a tempo *(ah TEM-poh)*   [It.] A tempo marking which indicates to return to the original tempo of a piece or section of music.

ABA form   A form in which an opening section (A) is followed by a contrasting section (B), which leads to the repetition of the opening section (A).

accelerando *(accel.) (ah-chel-leh-RAHN-doh)*   [It.] A tempo marking that indicates to gradually get faster.

accent   A symbol placed above or below a given note to indicate that the note should receive extra emphasis or stress. ( )

accidental   Any sharp, flat or natural that is not included in the key signature of a piece of music.

adagio *(ah-DAH-jee-oh)*   [It.] Slow tempo, but not as slow as *largo*.

ad libitum *(ad. lib.)*   [Lt.] An indication that the performer may vary the tempo or add or delete a vocal or instrumental part.

Aeolian scale *(ay-OH-lee-an)*   [Gk.] A modal scale that starts and ends on *la*. It is made up of the same arrangement of whole and half steps as a natural minor scale.

al fine *(ahl FEE-neh)*   [It.] To the end.

aleatory music *(AY-lee-uh-toh-ree)*   A type of music in which certain aspects are performed randomly. Also known as chance music.

alla breve   Indicates cut time; a duple meter in which there are two beats per measure, and the half note receives the beat. *See* cut time.

allargando (*allarg.*) (*ahl-ahr-GAHN-doh*) [It.] To broaden, become slower.

allegro (*ah-LEH-groh*) [It.] Brisk tempo; faster than *moderato*, slower than *vivace*.

allegro non troppo (*ah-LEH-groh nohn TROH-poh*) [It.] A tempo marking that indicates not too fast. Not as fast as *allegro*.

altered pitch Another name for an accidental.

alto (*AL-toh*) The lowest-sounding female voice.

andante (*ahn-DAHN- teh*) [It.] Moderately slow; a walking tempo.

andante con moto (*ahn-DAHN- teh kohn MOH-toh*) [It.] A slightly faster tempo, "with motion."

animato Quickly, lively; "animated."

anthem A choral composition in English using a sacred text.

arpeggio (*ahr-PEH-jee-oh*) [It.] A chord in which the pitches are sounded successively, usually from lowest to highest; in broken style.

arrangement A piece of music in which a composer takes an existing melody and adds extra features or changes the melody in some way.

arranger A composer who takes an original or existing melody and adds extra features or changes the melody in some way.

art song A musical setting of a poem.

articulation The amount of separation or connection between notes.

articulators The lips, teeth, tongue and other parts of the mouth and throat that are used to produce vocal sound.

avocational Not related to a job or career.

barbershop A style of *a cappella* singing in which three parts harmonize with the melody. The lead sings the melody while the tenor harmonizes above and the baritone and bass harmonize below.

barcarole A Venetian boat song.

baritone The male voice between tenor and bass.

barline A vertical line placed on the musical staff that groups notes and rests together.

Baroque period (*bah-ROHK*) [Fr.] The historical period in Western civilization from 1600 to 1750.

bass The lowest-sounding male voice.

bass clef A clef that generally indicates notes that sound lower than middle C.

basso continuo (*BAH-soh cun-TIN-you-oh*) [It.] A continually moving bass line, common in music from the Baroque period.

beat The steady pulse of music.

bebop style Popular in jazz, music that features notes that are light, lively and played quickly. Often the melodic lines are complex and follow unpredictable patterns.

blues scale An altered major scale that uses flatted or lowered third, fifth and seventh notes: *ma* (lowered from *mi*), *se* (lowered from *sol*) and *te* (lowered from *ti*).

blues style An original African American art form that developed in the early twentieth century in the Mississippi Delta region of the South. The lyrics often express feelings of frustration, hardship or longing. It often contains elements such as call and response, the blues scale and swing.

body percussion The use of one's body to make a percussive sound, such as clapping, snapping or stepping.

breath mark A symbol in vocal music used to indicate where a singer should take a breath. (,)

breath support A constant airflow necessary to produce sound for singing.

C

cadence A melodic or harmonic structure that marks the end of a phrase or the completion of a song.

call and response A derivative of the field hollers used by slaves as they worked. A leader or group sings a phrase (call) followed by a response of the same phrase by another group.

calypso A style of music that originated in the West Indies and which features syncopated rhythms and comical lyrics.

canon A musical form in which one part sings a melody, and the other parts sing the same melody, but enter at different times. Canons are sometimes called rounds.

cantabile *(con-TAH-bee-leh)* [It.] In a lyrical, singing style.

cantata *(con-TAH-tah)* [It.] A large-scale musical piece made up of several movements for singers and instrumentalists. Johann Sebastian Bach was a prominent composer of cantatas.

cantor *(CAN-tor)* A person who sings and/or teaches music in a temple or synagogue.

canzona [It.] A rhythmic instrumental composition that is light and fast-moving.

chamber music Music performed by a small instrumental ensemble, generally with one instrument per part. The string quartet is a popular form of chamber music, consisting of two violins, a viola and a cello. Chamber music was popular during the Classical period.

chantey *See* sea chantey.

chanteyman A soloist who improvised and led the singing of sea chanteys.

chest voice The lower part of the singer's vocal range.

chorale *(kuh-RAL)* [Gr.] Congregational song or hymn of the German Protestant Church.

chord The combination of three or more notes played or sung together at the same time.

chromatic scale *(kroh-MAT-tick)* [Gk.] A scale that consists of all half steps and uses all twelve pitches in an octave.

Classical period The historical period in Western civilization from 1750 to 1820.

clef The symbol at the beginning of a staff that indicates which lines and spaces represent which notes.

coda A special ending to a song. A concluding section of a composition. (⊕)

common time Another name for 4/4 meter. Also known as common meter. (**C**)

composer A person who takes a musical thought and writes it out in musical notation to share it with others.

compound meter Any meter in which the dotted quarter note receives the beat, and the division of the beat is based on three eighth notes. 6/8, 9/8 and 12/8 are examples of compound meter.

con moto *(kohn MOH-toh)* [It.] With motion.

concert etiquette A term used to describe what is appropriate behavior in formal or informal musical performances.

concerto *(cun-CHAIR-toh)* [Fr., It.] A composition for a solo instrument and orchestra.

concerto grosso *(cun-CHAIR-toh GROH-soh)* [Fr., It.] A multimovement Baroque piece for a group of soloists and an orchestra.

conductor A person who uses hand and arm gestures to interpret the expressive elements of music for singers and instrumentalists.

conductus A thirteenth-century song for two, three or four voices.

consonance Harmonies in chords or music that are pleasing to the ear.

Contemporary period The historical period from 1900 to the present.

countermelody A separate melodic line that supports and/or contrasts the melody of a piece of music.

counterpoint The combination of two or more melodic lines. The parts move independently while harmony is created. Johann Sebastian Bach is considered by many to be one of the greatest composers of contrapuntal music.

contrary motion A technique in which two melodic lines move in opposite directions.

crescendo *(creh-SHEN-doh)* [It.] A dynamic marking that indicates to gradually sing or play louder.

cut time Another name for 2/2 meter. (¢)

D
---

da capo *(D.C.) (dah KAH-poh)* [It.] Go back to the beginning and repeat; *see* also dal segno *and* al fine.

dal segno *(D.S.) (dahl SAYN-yah)* [It.] Go back to the sign and repeat.

D. C. al Fine *(FEE-nay)* [It.] A term that indicates to go back to the beginning and repeat. The term *al fine* indicates to sing to the end, or *fine.*

decrescendo *(DAY-creh-shen-doh)* [It.] A dynamic marking that indicates to gradually sing or play softer.

descant A special part in a piece of music that is usually sung higher than the melody or other parts of the song.

diatonic scale *(die-uh-TAH-nick)* A scale that uses no altered pitches or accidentals. Both the major scale and the natural minor scale are examples of a diatonic scale.

diction The pronunciation of words while singing.

diminished chord A minor chord in which the top note is lowered one half step from *mi* to *me.*

diminuendo *(dim.) (duh-min-yoo-WEN-doh)* [It.] Gradually getting softer; *see* decrescendo.

diphthong A combination of two vowel sounds.

dissonance A combination of pitches or tones that clash.

dolce *(DOHL-chay)* [It.] Sweetly.

dominant chord A chord built on the fifth note of a scale. In a major scale, this chord uses the notes *sol, ti* and *re,* and it may be called the **V** ("five") chord, since it is based on the fifth note of the major scale, or *sol.* In a minor scale, this chord uses the notes *mi, sol* and *ti* (or *mi, si* and *ti*), and it may be called the **v** or **V** ("five") chord, since it is based on the fifth note of the minor scale, or *mi.*

Dorian scale *(DOOR-ee-an)* [Gk.] A modal scale that starts and ends on *re.*

dot A symbol that increases the length of a given note by half its value. It is placed to the right of the note.

dotted half note A note that represents three beats of sound when the quarter note receives the beat. 𝅗𝅥.

double barline A set of two barlines that indicate the end of a piece or section of music.

D.S. al coda *(dahl SAYN-yoh ahl KOH-dah)* [It.] Repeat from the symbol (𝄋) and skip to the coda when you see the sign. (⊕)

duet A group of two singers or instrumentalists.

dynamics Symbols in music that indicate how loud or soft to sing or play.

E
---

eighth note A note that represents one half beat of sound when the quarter note receives the beat. Two eighth notes equal one beat of sound when the quarter note receives the beat. ♪ ♫

eighth rest A rest that represents one half beat of silence when the quarter note receives the beat. Two eighth rests equal one beat of silence when the quarter note receives the beat. 𝄾

expressive singing To sing with feeling.

falsetto [It.] The register in the male voice that extends far above the natural voice. The light upper range.

fermata *(fur-MAH-tah)* [It.] A symbol that indicates to hold a note or rest for longer than its given value. (⌒)

fine *(fee-NAY)* [It.] A term used to indicate the end of a piece of music.

flat A symbol that lowers the pitch of a given note by one half step.(♭)

folk music Music that passed down from generation to generation through oral tradition. Traditional music that reflects a place, event or a national feeling.

folk song A song passed down from generation to generation through oral tradition. A song that reflects a place, event or a national feeling.

form The structure or design of a musical composition.

forte *(FOR-tay)* [It.] A dynamic that indicates to sing or play loud. (*f*)

fortissimo *(for-TEE-see-moh)* [It.] A dynamic that indicates to sing or play very loud. (*ff*)

fugue *(FYOOG)* A musical form in which the same melody is performed by different instruments or voices entering at different times, thus adding layers of sound.

fusion Music that is developed by the act of combining various types and cultural influences of music into a new style.

gospel music Religious music that originated in the African American churches of the South. This music can be characterized by improvisation, syncopation and repetition.

grand staff A staff that is created when two staves are joined together.

grandioso [It.] Stately, majestic.

grave *(GRAH-veh)* [It.] Slow, solemn.

grazioso *(grah-tsee-OH-soh)* [It.] Graceful.

Gregorian chant A single, unaccompanied melodic line sung by male voices. Featuring a sacred text and used in the church, this style of music was developed in the Medieval period.

half note A note that represents two beats of sound when the quarter note receives the beat.

half rest A rest that represents two beats of silence when the quarter note receives the beat.

half step The smallest distance (interval) between two notes on a keyboard; the chromatic scale is composed entirely of half steps.

harmonic minor scale A minor scale that uses a raised seventh note, *si* (raised from *sol*).

harmonics Small whistle-like tones, or overtones, that are sometimes produced over a sustained pitch.

harmony A musical sound that is formed when two or more different pitches are played or sung at the same time.

head voice The higher part of the singer's vocal range.

homophonic *(hah-muh-FAH-nik)* [Gk.] A texture where all parts sing similar rhythm in unison or harmony.

homophony *(haw-MAW-faw-nee)* [Gk.] A type of music in which there are two or more parts with similar or identical rhythms being sung or played at the same time. Also, music in which melodic interest is concentrated in one voice part and may have subordinate accompaniment.

hushed A style marking indicating a soft, whispered tone.

imitation   The act of one part copying what another part has already played or sung.

improvisation   The art of singing or playing music, making it up as you go, or composing and performing a melody at the same time.

International Phonetic Alphabet (IPA)   A phonetic alphabet that provides a notational standard for all languages. Developed in Paris, France in 1886.

interval   The distance between two notes.

intonation   The accuracy of pitch, in-tune singing.

Ionian scale *(eye-OWN-ee-an)*   [Gk.] A modal scale that starts and ends on *do*. It is made up of the same arrangement of whole and half steps as a major scale.

jazz   An original American style of music that features swing rhythms, syncopation and improvisation.

jongleur   [Fr.] An entertainer who traveled from town to town during medieval times, often telling stories and singing songs.

key   Determined by a song's or scale's home tone, or keynote.

key signature   A symbol or set of symbols that determines the key of a piece of music.

ledger lines   Short lines that appear above, between treble and bass clefs, or below the bass clef, used to expand the notation.

legato *(leh-GAH-toh)*   [It.] A connected and sustained style of singing and playing.

lento *(LEN-toh)*   [It.] Slow; a little faster than *largo*, a little slower than *adagio*.

lied *(leet)*   [Ger.] A song in the German language, generally with a secular text.

liturgical text   A text that has been written for the purpose of worship in a church setting.

lute   An early form of the guitar.

Lydian scale *(LIH-dee-an)*   [Gk.] A modal scale that starts and ends on *fa*.

lyrics   The words of a song.

madrigal   A poem that has been set to music in the language of the composer. Featuring several imitative parts, it usually has a secular text and is generally sung *a cappella*.

maestoso *(mah-eh-STOH-soh)*   [It.] Perform majestically.

major chord   A chord that can be based on the *do*, *mi*, and *sol* of a major scale.

major scale   A scale that has *do* as its home tone, or keynote. It is made up of a specific arrangement of whole steps and half steps in the following order: W + W + H + W + W + W + H.

major tonality   A song that is based on a major scale with *do* as its keynote, or home tone.

mangulina   A traditional dance from the Dominican Republic.

marcato *(mar-CAH-toh)*   [It.] A stressed and accented style of singing and playing.

mass A religious service of prayers and ceremonies originating in the Roman Catholic church consisting of spoken and sung sections. It consists of several sections divided into two groups: proper (text changes for every day) and ordinary (text stays the same in every mass). Between the years 1400 and 1600, the mass assumed its present form consisting of the Kyrie, Gloria, Credo, Sanctus and Agnus Dei. It may include chants, hymns and psalms as well. The mass also developed into large musical works for chorus, soloists and even orchestra.

measure The space between two barlines.

Medieval period The historical period in Western civilization also known as the Middle Ages (400–1430).

medley A collection of songs musically linked together.

melisma *(muh-LIZ-mah)* [Gk.] A group of notes sung to a single syllable or word.

melismatic singing *(muh-liz-MAT-ik)* [Gk.] A style of text setting in which one syllable is sung over many notes.

melodic contour The overall shape of the melody.

melodic minor scale A minor scale that uses raised sixth and seventh notes: *fi* (raised from *fa*) and *si* (raised from *sol*). Often, these notes are raised in ascending patterns, but not in descending patterns.

melody A logical succession of musical tones.

meter A way of organizing rhythm.

meter signature See *time signature*.

metronome marking A sign that appears over the top line of the staff at the beginning of a piece or section of music that indicates the tempo. It shows the kind of note that will receive the beat and the number of beats per minute as measured by a metronome.

mezzo forte *(MEH-tsoh FOR tay)* [It.] A dynamic that indicates to sing or play medium loud. (*mf*)

mezzo piano *(MEH-tsoh pee-AH-noh)* [It.] A dynamic that indicates to sing or play medium soft. (*mp*)

mezzo voce *(MEH-tsoh VOH-cheh)* [It.] With half voice; reduced volume and tone.

minor chord A chord that can be based on the *la, do,* and *mi* of a minor scale.

minor scale A scale that has *la* as its home tone, or keynote. It is made up of a specific arrangement of whole steps and half steps in the following order: W + H +W + W + H + W + W.

minor tonality A song that is based on a minor scale with *la* as its keynote, or home tone.

mixed meter A technique in which the time signature or meter changes frequently within a piece of music.

Mixolydian scale *(mix-oh-LIH-dee-an)* [Gr.] A modal scale that starts and ends on *sol*.

modal scale A scale based on a mode. Like major and minor scales, each modal scale is made up of a specific arrangement of whole steps and half steps, with the half steps occurring between *mi* and *fa*, and *ti* and *do*.

mode An early system of pitch organization that was used before major and minor scales and keys were developed.

modulation A change in the key or tonal center of a piece of music within the same song.

molto [It.] Very or much; for example, *molto rit.* means "much slower."

motet *(moh-teht)* Originating as a Medieval and Renaissance polyphonic song, this choral form of composition became an unaccompanied work, often in contrapuntal style. Also, a short, sacred choral piece with a Latin text that is used in religious services but is not a part of the regular mass.

motive A shortened expression, sometimes contained within a phrase.

music critic A writer who gives an evaluation of a musical performance.

music notation Any means of writing down music, including the use of notes, rests and symbols.

musical A play or film whose action and dialogue are combined with singing and dancing.

musical theater An art form that combines acting, singing, and dancing to tell a story. It often includes staging, costumes, lighting and scenery.

mysterioso [It.] Perform in a mysterious or haunting way; to create a haunting mood.

N

narrative song A song that tells a story.

national anthem A patriotic song adopted by nations through tradition or decree.

nationalism Patriotism; pride of country. This feeling influenced many Romantic composers such as Wagner, Tchaikovsky, Dvorák, Chopin and Brahms.

natural A symbol that cancels a previous sharp or flat, or a sharp or flat in a key signature. (♮)

natural minor scale A minor scale that uses no altered pitches or accidentals.

no breath mark A direction not to take a breath at a specific place in the composition. (N.B.)

non troppo (nahn TROH-poh) [It.] Not too much; for example, allegro non troppo, "not too fast."

notation Written notes, symbols and directions used to represent music within a composition.

O

octave An interval of two pitches that are eight notes apart on a staff.

ode A poem written in honor of a special person or occasion. These poems were generally dedicated to a member of a royal family. In music, an ode usually includes several sections for choir, soloists and orchestra.

opera A combination of singing, instrumental music, dancing and drama that tells a story.

optional divisi (opt.div.) Indicating a split in the music into optional harmony, shown by a smaller cued note.

oral tradition Music that is learned through rote or by ear and is interpreted by its performer(s).

oratorio (or-uh-TOR-ee-oh) [It.] A dramatic work for solo voices, chorus and orchestra presented without theatrical action. Usually, oratorios are based on a literary or religious theme.

ostinato (ahs-tuh-NAH-toh) [It.] A rhythmic or melodic passage that is repeated continuosly.

overture A piece for orchestra which serves as an introduction to an opera or other dramatic work.

P

palate The roof of the mouth; the hard palate is at the front, the soft palate is at the back.

parallel motion A technique in which two or more melodic lines move in the same direction.

parallel sixths A group of intervals that are a sixth apart and which move at the same time and in the same direction.

parallel thirds A group of intervals that are a third apart and which move at the same time and in the same direction.

part-singing Two or more parts singing an independent melodic line at the same time.

patsch The act of slapping one's hands on one's thighs.

pentatonic scale A five-tone scale using the pitches do, re, mi, sol and la.

perfect fifth An interval of two pitches that are five notes apart on a staff.

perfect fourth An interval of two pitches that are four notes apart on a staff.

phrase A musical idea with a beginning and an end.

Phrygian scale *(FRIH-gee-an)* [Gk.] A modal scale that starts and ends on *mi*.

pianissimo *(pee-ah-NEE-see-moh)* [It.] A dynamic that indicates to sing or play very soft. *(pp)*

piano *(pee-AH-noh)* [It.] A dynamic that indicates to sing or play soft. *(p)*

pitch Sound, the result of vibration; the highness or lowness of a tone, determined by the number of vibrations per second.

pitch matching In a choral ensemble, the ability to sing the same notes as those around you.

piu *(pew)* [It.] More; for example, *piu forte* means "more loudly."

poco *(POH-koh)* [It.] Little; for example *poco dim.* means "a little softer."

poco a poco *(POH-koh ah POH-koh)* [It.] Little by little; for example, *poco a poco cresc.* means "little by little increase in volume."

polyphony *(pah-LIH-fun-nee)* [Gk.] Literally, "many sounding." A type of music in which there are two or more different melodic lines being sung or played at the same time. Polyphony was refined during the Renaissance, and this period is sometimes called "golden age of polyphony."

polyrhythms A technique in which several different rhythms are performed at the same time.

presto *(PREH-stoh)* [It.] Very fast.

program music A descriptive style of music composed to relate or illustrate a specific incident, situation or drama; the form of the piece is often dictated or influenced by the nonmusical program. This style commonly occurs in music composed during the Romantic period.

Q

quarter note A note that represents one beat of sound when the quarter note receives the beat.

quarter rest A rest that represents one beat of silence when the quarter note receives the beat.

quartet A group of four singers or instrumentalists.

R

rallentando *(rall.)* *(rahl-en-TAHN-doh)* [It.] Meaning to "perform more and more slowly." *See also ritard.*

refrain A repeated section at the end of each phrase or verse in a song. Also known as a chorus.

register, vocal A term used for different parts of the singer's range, such as head register, or head voice (high notes); and chest register, or chest voice (low notes).

relative minor scale A minor scale that shares the same key signature as its corresponding major scale. Both scales share the same half steps, between *mi* and *fa*, and *ti* and *do*.

Renaissance period The historical period in Western civilization from 1430 to 1600.

repeat sign A symbol that indicates that a section of music should be repeated. (:‖)

repetition The restatement of a musical idea; repeated pitches; repeated "A" section in ABA form.

requiem *(REK-wee-ehm)* [Lt.] Literally, "rest." A mass written and performed to honor the dead and comfort the living.

resonance Reinforcement and intensification of sound by vibration.

rest A symbol used in music notation to indicate silence.

rhythm The combination of long and short notes and rests in music. These may move with the beat, faster than the beat or slower than the beat.

ritard *(rit.)* *(ree-TAHRD)* [It.] A tempo marking that indicates to gradually get slower.

Romantic period The historical period in Western civilization from 1820 to 1900.

rondo form A form in which a repeated section is separated by several contrasting sections.

rote The act of learning a song by hearing it over and over again.

round *See* canon.

rubato *(roo-BAH-toh)* [It.] The freedom to slow down and/or speed up the tempo without changing the overall pulse of a piece of music.

S

sacred music Music associated with religious services or themes.

scale A group of pitches that are sung or played in succession and are based on a particular home tone, or keynote.

scat singing An improvisational style of singing that uses nonsense syllables instead of words. It was made popular by jazz trumpeter Louis Armstrong.

sea chantey A song sung by sailors, usually in rhythm with their work.

secular music Music not associated with religious services or themes.

sempre *(SEHM-preh)* [It.] Always, continually.

sempre accelerando *(sempre accel.)* *(SEHM-preh ahk-chel)* [It.] A term that indicates to gradually increase the tempo of a piece or section of music.

sequence A successive musical pattern that begins on a higher or lower pitch each time it is repeated.

serenata [It.] A large-scale musical work written in honor of a special occasion. Generally performed in the evening or outside, it is often based on a mythological theme.

sforzando *(sfohr-TSAHN-doh)* [It.] A sudden strong accent on a note or chord. (*sfz*)

sharp A symbol that raises the pitch of a given note one half step.

shekere An African shaker consisting of a hollow gourd surrounded by beads.

sight-sing Reading and singing music at first sight.

simile *(sim.)* *(SIM-ee-leh)* [It.] To continue the same way.

simple meter Any meter in which the quarter note receives the beat, and the division of the beat is based on two eighth notes. 2/4, 3/4 and 4/4 are examples of simple meter.

singing posture The way one sits or stands while singing.

sixteenth note A note that represents one quarter beat of sound when the quarter note receives the beat. Four sixteenth notes equal one beat of sound when the quarter note receives the beat.

sixteenth rest A rest that represents one quarter beat of silence when the quarter note receives the beat. Four sixteenth rests equal one beat of silence when the quarter note receives the beat.

skipwise motion The movement from a given note to another note that is two or more notes above or below it on the staff.

slur A curved line placed over or under a group of notes to indicate that they are to be performed without a break.

solfège syllables Pitch names using *do, re, mi, fa, sol, la, ti, do*, etc.

solo One person singing or playing an instrument alone.

sonata-allegro form A large ABA form consisting of three sections: exposition, development and recapitulation. This form was made popular during the Classical period.

soprano The highest-sounding female voice.

sostenuto *(SAHS-tuh-noot-oh)* [It.] The sustaining of a tone or the slackening of tempo.

sotto voce In a quiet, subdued manner; "under" the voice.

spirito *(SPEE-ree-toh)* [It.] Spirited; for example, *con spirito* ("with spirit").

spiritual Songs that were first sung by African American slaves, usually based on biblical themes or stories.

staccato *(stah-KAH-toh)* [It.] A short and detached style of singing or playing.

staff A series of five horizontal lines and four spaces on which notes are written. A staff is like a ladder. Notes placed higher on the staff sound higher than notes placed lower on the staff.

stage presence A performer's overall appearance on stage, including enthusiasm, facial expression and posture.

staggered breathing In ensemble singing, the practice of planning breaths so that no two singers take a breath at the same time, thus creating the overall effect of continuous singing.

staggered entrances A technique in which different parts and voices enter at different times.

stanza A section in a song in which the words change on each repeat. Also known as a verse.

step-wise motion The movement from a given note to another note that is directly above or below it on the staff.

strophe A verse or stanza in a song.

strophic A form in which the melody repeats while the words change from verse to verse.

style The particular character of a musical work; often indicated by words at the beginning of a composition, telling the performer the general manner in which the piece is to be performed.

subdominant chord A chord built on the fourth note of a scale. In a major scale, this chord uses the notes *fa, la* and *do*, and it may be called the **IV** ("four") chord, since it is based on the fourth note of the major scale, or *fa*. In a minor scale, this chord uses the notes *re, fa* and *la*, and it may be called the **iv** ("four") chord, since it is based on the fourth note of the minor scale, or *re*.

subito (sub.) *(SOO-bee-toh)* [It.] Suddenly.

suspension The holding over of one or more musical tones in a chord into the following chord, producing a momentary discord.

swing rhythms Rhythms in which the second eighth note of each beat is played or sung like the last third of triplet, creating an uneven, "swing" feel. A style often found in jazz and blues. Swing rhythms are usually indicated at the beginning of a song or section.

syllabic See *syllabic singing*.

syllabic singing A style of text setting in which one syllable is sung on each note.

syllabic stress The stressing of one syllable over another.

symphonic poem A single-movement work for orchestra, inspired by a painting, play or other literary or visual work. Franz Liszt was a prominent composer of symphonic poems. Also known as a tone poem.

symphony A large-scale work for orchestra.

syncopation The placement of accents on a weak beat or a weak portion of the beat, or on a note or notes that normally do not receive extra emphasis.

synthesizer A musical instrument that produces sounds electronically, rather than by the physical vibrations of an acoustic instrument.

T

tempo   Terms in music that indicate how fast or slow to sing or play.

tempo I or tempo primo   *See* a tempo.

tenor   The highest-sounding male voice.

tenuto *(teh-NOO-toh)*   [It.] A symbol placed above or below a given note indicating that the note should receive stress and/or that its value should be slightly extended.

text   Words, usually set in a poetic style, that express a central thought, idea or narrative.

texture   The thickness of the different layers of horizontal and vertical sounds.

theme   A musical idea, usually a melody.

theme and variation form   A musical form in which variations of the basic theme make up the composition.

third   An interval of two pitches that are three notes apart on a staff.

tie   A curved line used to connect two or more notes of the same pitch together in order to make one longer note.

tied notes   Two or more notes of the same pitch connected together with a tie in order to make one longer note.

timbre   The tone quality of a person's voice or musical instrument.

time signature   The set of numbers at the beginning of a piece of music. The top number indicates the number of beats per measure. The bottom number indicates the kind of note that receives the beat. Time signature is sometimes called meter signature.

to coda   Skip to (⊕) or CODA.

tone color   That which distinguishes the voice or tone of one singer or instrument from another; for example, a soprano from an alto, or a flute from a clarinet. *See also* timbre.

tonic chord   A chord built on the home tone, or keynote of a scale. In a major scale, this chord uses the notes *do, mi* and *sol*, and it may be called the **I** ("one") chord, since it is based on the first note of the major scale, or *do*. In a minor scale, this chord uses the notes *la, do* and *mi*, and it may be called the **i** ("one") chord, since it is based on the first note of the minor scale, or *la*.

treble clef   A clef that generally indicates notes that sound higher than middle C.

trio   A group of three singers or instrumentalists with usually one on a part.

triplet   A group of notes in which three notes of equal duration are sung in the time normally given to two notes of equal duration.

troppo *(TROHP-oh)*   [It.] Too much; for example, *allegro non troppo* ("not too fast").

tutti *(TOO-tee)*   [It.] Meaning "all" or "together."

twelve-tone music   A type of music that uses all twelve tones of the scale equally. Developed in the early twentieth century, Arnold Schoenberg is considered to be the pioneer of this style of music.

two-part music   A type of music in which two different parts are sung or played.

U

unison   All parts singing or playing the same notes at the same time.

V

variation   A modification of a musical idea, usually after its initial appearance in a piece.

vivace *(vee-VAH-chay)*   [It.] Very fast; lively.

vocal jazz   A popular style of music characterized by strong prominent meter, improvisation and dotted or syncopated patterns. Sometimes sung *a cappella.*

whole note A note that represents four beats of sound when the quarter note receives the beat. o

whole rest A rest that represents four beats of silence when the quarter note receives the beat. ▬

whole step The combination of two successive half steps.

word painting A technique in which the music reflects the meaning of the words.

word stress The act of singing important parts of the text in a more accented style than the other parts.

yoik A vocal tradition of the Sámi people of the Arctic region of Sampi that features short melodic phrases that are repeated with slight variations.

Classified Index

Index of Songs and Spotlights

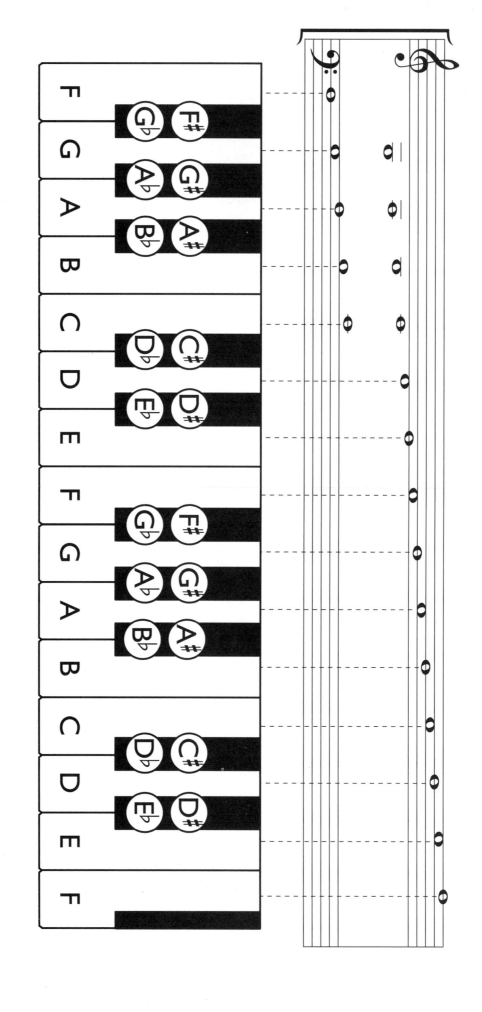